In the Shelter

In the Shelter

Shelter

finding a home in the world

Pádraig Ó Tuama

foreword by Krista Tippett

BROADLEAF BOOKS

MINNEAPOLIS

IN THE SHELTER
Finding a Home in the World

First published in Great Britain in 2015 by Hodder & Stoughton, A Hachette UK company

Unless credited otherwise, poems © Pádraig Ó Tuama

The right of Pádraig Ó Tuama to be identified as the Author of the Work has been asserted by him in accordance with the Copyright, Designs and Patents Act 1988.

Unless indicated otherwise, Scripture quotations are from the New Revised Standard Version of the Bible, © copyright 1989, 1995 by the Division of Christian Education of the National Council of Churches of Christ in the United States of America and are by permission. All rights reserved.

Every reasonable effort has been made to trace the copyright holders, but if there are any errors or omissions, the publisher would be pleased to insert the appropriate acknowledgment in any subsequent printings or editions.

Cover image: Gus Design / shutterstock
Cover design: Cindy Laun

Print ISBN: 978-1-5064-7052-8
eBook ISBN: 978-1-5064-7053-5

Do Paul, grá mo chroí,
agus Ruth Hockey, cara croíúil.

Contents

Bíonn siúlach scéalach.
Travelers have tales to tell.

♀

Where you stumble, there lies your treasure. The very cave you are afraid to enter turns out to be the source of what you are looking for. The damned thing in the cave, that was so dreaded, has become the center.

Joseph Campbell

♀

How we spend our days is, of course, how we spend our lives.

Annie Dillard

♀

Gloria Dei est vivens homo.

Irenaeus of Lyons

Foreword

This book has been passed hand to hand during tumultuous years in the life of the world. To say that it is one of the most beautiful and quietly necessary books of our young century is a sweeping assertion, but I will make it. This is an exquisite work of spiritual autobiography. It is an original offering of theological and sacred reflection on meanings of belonging, home, and welcome. It is an extraordinary introduction to a biblical way of thinking and questioning, a Christian way of seeing and being. Yet it is presented so winsomely and wisely that—like every spiritual classic—it offers its riches to the secular as to the devout. Pádraig Ó Tuama takes the reader's hand and walks us lyrically through his own loss, confusion, despair, joys, and learning. With softness and firmness intertwined, he shows us how to do this with generosity toward ourselves and the others with whom we share life.

The varied fields in which he is an esteemed practitioner—religion, poetry, and conflict mediation—make this a holistic text for navigating the shadows and potentialities that we meet in our life together as in ourselves. But it is the rich, reverent, contagious love of words that binds these various passions and makes this book a delight. The Irish tongue is a character in the book. Pádraig dances with language while he is demanding of it and insists that we should be too. For we so easily "bruise" others with our words in the course of a day and are bruised. The names we give to things sanctify and reveal their contradictions. It may be more important to get the right people into the room, he observes—and what an observation—than to get the right words into the room.

Such insights convince because they have emerged in bitter crucibles of his life. His country was still at war when he was born, and the Irish language that we come to love through reading this book was nearly extinguished. Pádraig endured exorcisms and exile as a young gay man born in a most traditional Catholic culture. He knows "the burden of survival" but more: "I understand that hope can break you." Yet what astonishes, and teaches most profoundly, is the capacity he develops to claim his inheritance—his right to be, his gift to offer—in places that have not wanted him. Not to define his country, his neighbors, or his church because of how they have defined and sought to diminish him. He pursues what is life-giving in all of those places and shows us the presence and practice that requires.

The simplest definition of theology is etymological: words about God. Like all the best theology across the ages, Pádraig's words that point at God point back to who we are and can be. And in the best tradition of the biblical and social prophets across time, his disarming use of language cracks open the reader's imagination, revealing old formulations that have kept us numb. None of us, if truth be told, knows home, belonging, and welcome—tangible or spiritual—without struggle. Indeed, the meaning of—and the means to—these experiences are aching, wide-open questions at the center of twenty-first-century shifts and ruptures. Belonging "creates and undoes us both. If spirituality does not speak to this power, then it speaks to little."

I have given this book to young colleagues and to great religious minds, to atheist and Buddhist friends, to my children. Read this, they all affirm with me, and tread more softly, courageously, and self-forgivingly—all at once—through our hurting, hoping world and the heartbreaking, heart-opening frontier that is a human life.

Krista Tippett

Hello to the world

I didn't grow up in a city, but I was born on the edges of one. My parents moved to the countryside when I was five, so I learned to love fields and long walks. But I always loved the idea of the city.

The word "city" comes from the Old French *cité*, which itself comes from the Latin word *civis*, from which we get the word "citizen." The world is in the citizen, whether the citizen is in the city or the forest. But I, taking long walks nightly in the country, longed to be in the city, because there I hoped I could meet the worlds that the country couldn't contain.

Of course, when I moved to the city, I found that the city couldn't contain those worlds either. I met a Finnish woman once who had spent years dreaming of moving to Dublin. When she got there, she was initially distracted, but then, after a while, she said that she realized that she brought her self with herself, and no city was big enough to meet that.

Once, I was in New York City. For ten years I'd imagined that I would become a priest there. When I finally managed to visit the city, it took ten minutes to realize that my plans would change. I didn't like the priests, and they wouldn't like me. But I loved the city. I was left with a question: What do I do now?

I walked the city.

In the Shelter

I walked until I got lost, and when I was totally lost, I went down into the subway and took a train and felt even more lost. Eventually I found my way to the subway underneath Grand Central Station. I had nowhere to be, and hours to waste, and I couldn't make my mind up about what to do—either with the day or with my life. Both seemed open and both were intimidating. I heard some music from a side of the station and went to look. In the corner was a woman. She was wearing a dress and fancy shoes and a coat and a small hat. Her face was clear and bright, and she was singing along to recorded music. It must have been a well-known church song, because all of the others around her were joining in with the chorus, a chorus that just repeated "Alleluia" over and over, like a jazzy psalm. She had a lovely voice and moved with style and rhythm, smiling and singing and repeating "Alleluia."

Alleluia, Alleluia.

I didn't feel like singing, but she was so full of life that I couldn't leave. She was singing about the woman in John's Gospel who makes her way to the well during the hottest time of the day and, at the well, meets Jesus. It's a story I love, because the characters are so rich and lively. When Jesus asks her to draw some water for him, she tells him he shouldn't be speaking to her. When he says she should ask him for the water of life, she says that he has no bucket. They speak anyway, and she discovers herself in the words of a stranger.

So there I was, in the belly of the city, hearing songs about a story that I loved on a day when everything seemed to be dying. I was the only white boy surrounded by Black women twice my age, and they were singing "Alleluia," and I was crying and thinking that maybe everything wasn't lost anyway.

2

Hello to the city.

Hello to the little worlds we live in.

Another time in another city, I was walking at nighttime. It was Melbourne, a city that was my home for four years. It was dark, and as I was walking toward Flinders Street train station, I saw a man who seemed distressed. I stopped to ask if he wanted directions, and as he replied, it was clear that he was Deaf. I owned a Sign Language dictionary and had perused it for years, and so I was delighted to practice my limited knowledge. He told me he was French and had only arrived in the city that day. I spelled I-r-i-s-h, and he asked me how I knew sign language, and I got lost in the spelling. He was looking for the train station, and I said to come with me.

We walked, and I stumbled through his fluent language. He was happy to have met someone who could speak a few words of his language, and I was delighted at the happy chance to talk. He was pure charm. At one point, I was trying to say something in sign, and he laughed and did an imitation of my cumbersome signing. When we said goodbye at the train station, he grabbed both of my slow hands in his, and I felt his warmth and fluency, and we shared a joy of being human in the city.

Earlier on that night, I'd been walking around the city and someone had come up to me and asked if I knew the truth of Jesus Christ. I told him I wasn't interested, but he must have reckoned that a refusal is an engagement, so he persisted. I even told him that I had a Bible in my bag and that, on good days, I tried to read it, and he asked me whether I had the proper translation of the Bible in my bag.

3

In the Shelter

He asked me to say a prayer with him, but I wouldn't. I've lied enough in my life.

The reason I was walking the city late at night was because only two days before I had received a phone call from my mother. We always spoke on a Sunday night. It was winter in Melbourne, so there was a nine-hour difference between Ireland and Australia. My mother's phone call came at the wrong time. My childhood best friend was dead, she told me, dead from suicide, and then there was nothing else to say. Nothing else. He'd taken his life and his sadness and his burdens and his body and hung them all in a place where we used to play. So I'd done the only thing I knew to do. I went to the city and I walked in the city. At one point I walked into a bookshop and found *The Lord of the Rings*, a book I love. I turned to the place where Gandalf is dead. The bereaved companions have found their way to Lothlórien, and on the first night, they hear the others sing laments for the Wizard. The laments are in Elvish, and when some ask Legolas, the Elf, to translate, he refuses, saying that the grief was too near, a matter for tears and not yet for song.

I read it over and over and over, standing at a bookshelf, holding a heavy book, in a shop in the middle of the city.

Hello to the need for shelter.

Hello to the stories that shelter us.

4

Narrative Theology # 1

And I said to him:
Are there answers to all of this?
And he said:
The answer is in a story
and the story is being told.

And I said:
But there is so much pain
And she answered, plainly:
Pain will happen.

Then I said:
Will I ever find meaning?
And they said:
You will find meaning
where you give meaning.

The answer is in a story
and the story isn't finished.

1

Hello to here

When traveling, I carry three books, one each of poetry, fiction, and religion. I also bring a diary. In 1998, everything fell apart. At that stage, I had been ill for a year—dizziness, aching, exhaustion, insomnia, nausea—and I was finding it impossible to hold it together. I didn't know what to do. My friend Wendy said, "I'm driving to France. Do you want to come?" I'd had to leave my job because I was too ill, and now, while I didn't have much money, I had enough for a few months. So for no reason other than it was the first idea in a year that had felt good, I went. I went with some clothes, a book of poetry, a book of religion, and a book of fiction, and I ended up in Taizé, that little monastery in eastern France known for generosity and light.

It was spring, and I stayed in the house of silence at Taizé. I was there with twenty other men. It was a sunny Lent. I enjoyed bites of chocolate in small buns of bread for breakfast and showed up for prayer and reflection. "During your weeks in silence here, don't spend too much of your time reading," one of the Taizé brothers said. "Make sure you spend time in silence and stillness."

In the Shelter

I read *The Lord of the Rings* in a week.

It wasn't my first time reading it. You could call it rhythm or habit, but I've always reread books, sometimes rebeginning the first page once the last page has ended. For years, I accompanied exam time with readings from Middle Earth, because the anxiety of exams was calmed by the richness of Sam's courage. So in France, it was no surprise that I had put Tolkien in the bag I'd packed. I was standing in what felt like the ruin of myself, and I had brought a fiction to hold me together. It was a good fiction, and it worked. It held me together.

I had a copy of the Bible too, but I was doubting my decision to bring it. I didn't feel like I could read it—I felt that I could read it if I were someone else, someone more holy, healthy, and heterosexual. I felt caged in by my readings of the Bible, so it lay in the bag with the wool sweaters, underwear, and guilt I'd packed.

Tolkien wrote, "I have claimed that Escape is one of the main functions of fairy-stories, and since I do not disapprove of them, it is plain that I do not accept the tone of scorn or pity with which 'Escape' is now so often used. Why should a man be scorned if, finding himself in prison, he tries to get out and go home? Or if he cannot do so, he thinks and talks about other topics than jailers and prison-walls?" I was, in a sense, wanting to escape a religious belief that said I shouldn't be ill, I couldn't be gay, and I couldn't go on. And so, in a monastery, surrounded by rules, silence, and four-part harmonies, I was finding myself in some kind of prison. I did what made the most sense at the time: I turned to myth. Myth is, after all, what is more than true.

Hello to here

My favorite poem from David Wagoner is "Lost":

> Stand still. The trees ahead and bushes beside you
> Are not lost. Wherever you are is called Here
> And you must treat it as a powerful stranger.

The truth of this poem is an old truth. There are the places you wish to go, there are the places you desperately wish you never left, there are the places you imagine you should be, and there is the place called here. In the world of Wagoner's poem, it is the rooted things—trees and bushes—that tell the truth to the person who is lost, the person with legs and fear who wishes to be elsewhere. The person must stand still, feel their body still on the ground where they are, in order to learn the wisdom. This is not easy wisdom; it is frightening wisdom. In Irish, there is a phrase, *ar eagla na heagla*, that translates as "for fear of fear." It is true that there are some things that we fear but that there is, even deeper, a fear of fear. So we are prevented from being here not only by being frightened of certain places but by the fear of being frightened of certain places. So "Stand still," the poet advises. Learn from the things that are already in the place where you wish you were not.

Hello to the fear of fear.

Hello to here.

In the Shelter

Anyway, it was Easter week. In Taizé, we had morning reflections of about ten minutes each, every morning. We had a monk there who could deliver his short talks in English, French, German, or Spanish. He would ask, moving casually from language to language, which tongues he should use in order to be understood by everyone. He translated himself with ease, and his English was as rich in poetry as his French. On Holy Thursday—the day that we should have been reading about the Last Supper—he instead turned to a reading for Easter Sunday. He turned to the Gospel of John, particularly reading the text where Jesus arrives in the upper room wherein the disciples had locked themselves for fear. The Taizé monk read the text, asked someone else to read it in Dutch, someone else in Norwegian, and then he noted that when Jesus arrived in that room of fear, he greeted his disciples by saying, "Peace be with you."

Part of the concern in rereading a text often is that in so doing, you read less and recognize more. You glide over familiar words. Or to be more particular, you glide over familiar presumptions, and so, with time, you aren't reading what's there; you're reading what you think is there.

Hello to here

The Taizé brother suggested that we pause for a moment and consider the words "Peace be with you," which the resurrected Jesus says to his locked-in followers. The Taizé brother said that, in a real sense, we can read that as "Hello." After all, it's the standard greeting in Hebrew, Arabic, and Aramaic. He smiled and asked us all to say hello in our own language. There were many languages in the room. Then we approached the text again.

The disciples were there, in fear, in an upper room, locked away, and suddenly the one they had abandoned and perhaps the one they most feared to be with them was with them, and he said hello.

Hello to you in this locked room.

♥

In many circles of faith or spirituality, there is generous time given to the testimony—the telling of the story of conversion or reconversion, of enlightenment or change. It is a moving thing, to listen to the testimony. But testimony, if told or heard unwisely, can be a colonization of a single experience into a universal requirement. Jesus fed me when I was hungry, we hear, and those who are hungry feel bereft. Jesus healed me when I was sick, say the healthy, and the burdened feel more burdened. Meditation cured me of depression, say some, and others make plans to hide the Prozac. Upon whom is the burden of words? I don't know. I don't think there is an answer. I cannot dampen gladness because it will burden the unglad. But I cannot proclaim gladness as a promise that will only shackle the already bound. Faith shelters some, and it shadows others. It loosens some, and it binds others. Is this a judgment of the message or the messenger, the one praying or the prayer prayed? I don't know.

Hello to what we do not know.

What I do know is that it can help to find the words to tell the truth of where you are now. If you can find the courage to name "here"—especially in the place where you do not wish to be—it can help you be there. Instead of resenting another's words of gladness or pain, it may be possible to hear it as simply another location. They are there and I am here. At another point, we will be in different locations, and everybody will pass by many locations in their life. The pain is only deepened when the location is resented or, even worse, unnamed.

Hello to here.

♀

By the time I arrived with my bag and my books at Taizé, my relationship with religion had worsened my sense of my self. At that point, my relationships with others were guided by what I now recognize as desperation. "Could you like me?" I asked over and over and over. I asked it of friends, I asked it of colleagues, I was desperate to ask it of authority and to beg for acceptance from the God that I was trying to love.

Somehow, in the simplicity of that moment in a monastery in France, something became clear. I might be locked in somewhere, I might be looking to Middle Earth to save me, but I could do something else, something altogether brave and simple. I could begin to greet the truth, to greet the "here" of now. This required me to recognize that I might have to ask myself some questions and that I would need to tell myself some truthful answers.

That day, I skipped the morning prayer and the afternoon prayer. I walked and found that I was able—for the first time in years—to tell the truth to myself without shame.

I am falling apart.

♀

I was, like so many people, able to face truths about home only when I was someone foreign. I was an Irishman in France, moving between English and school French and processing phrases in Irish. I was writing about loneliness one day—oh, the time available!—and I realized that the word for "loneliness" in Irish—*uaigneach*—shares a root with the word for "grave"—*uaigh*. And another day, while listening to a talk from one of the Taizé monks, I realized that I was repeating, round and round and round like the Hail Mary, the French words *je me déteste*. I hate myself. Or, at least, that's what I wanted to say. I knew that the adverb *me* went before the verb, but I busied myself wondering if I'd translated the phrase correctly because I wasn't sure that the French *me* could both be "me" and "myself."

What does it mean when you interrupt self-loathing to consider the grammatical conjugation of the words you're using to abhor yourself?

It means that words have power.

In the Shelter

So anyway, there I was, a lonely youngster with languages, longing, and the love of God all haunting me. I was beginning to greet a place called here. There was a lot to greet, and I'd only just begun.

Hello to time.

◉

At the end of the Gospel of John, the narrator says that if everything done by Jesus of Nazareth were to be written down then the world itself would not contain the books. James Joyce tried to write the world of a day, and the book is very, very thick and very, very long. How long would the book of our day be? How many chapters can describe mundanity? How many words are needed to tunnel along the radius to the heart? And how many words to climb back to the skin?

I had come to Taizé with some clothes, a book of myth, a book of poetry, a book for writing in, and the books of the Bible. I was using the first three with regularity and relief. I was seriously considering abandoning the Bible because my readings of it caused such anxiety. One day, I found myself asking myself why, if I disliked it so much, I had it with me. I didn't know the answer, but I knew that sometimes, read in a certain light, I found the heart swelling with courage. I knew that when the brother in Taizé spoke, I found space for my own life, and I knew that somehow, if I could only settle into a different reading of truth, I could find in prayer words both generous and fierce.

Hello to here

I remember reading through an old *National Geographic* magazine. There was a story in it about a photojournalist who was returning, after many years' absence, to Papua New Guinea, where she'd grown up. She had taken pictures of a remote area of jungle. When she'd lived there as a child, her parents had worked—as medics, or missionaries, I forget the details—among a nomadic tribal group who moved between different homelands depending on the season. She recalled the language of her youth, a language she had learned from her friends. There was no word for "hello" in this local language in Papua New Guinea. Instead, upon seeing someone, one simply said, "You are here."

The answer, as I recall it, was equally straightforward: "Yes I am."

Whether by fact or fiction, it remains that for decades I have thought of the words "You are here" and "Yes I am" as good places to begin something that might be called prayer.

Where is it that we are when we pray? We are, obviously, in the place where we are. However, we are often in many places. We are saying to ourselves, "I should be somewhere else" or "I should be someone else" or "I am not where I say I am." In prayer, to begin where you are not is a poor beginning. To begin where you are may take courage, or compromise, or painful truth telling. Whatever it

15

takes, it's wise to begin there. The only place to begin is where I am, and whether by desire or disaster, I am here. My being here is not dependent on my recognition of the fact. I am here anyway. But it might help if I could learn to look around.

♀

In the sixth chapter of the Gospel of John, Jesus feeds a hungry crowd, using some bread offered by a small boy. Then he leaves and a storm comes.

The events, often told separately, seem to me to be part of a broad storyboard about absence, presence, and the changing nature of circumstance.

Initially, Jesus is on a mountainside. The Gospel writer makes sure to note that there were a great number of people and a great deal of grass. The people are hungry, and a small boy offers bread. The people are made to sit on the grass, and somehow, when the boy's bread is shared, there is enough for them all. It is, in a certain sense, a picnic. Much time can be spent wondering whether it was a miraculous multiplication of the small boy's small offering or whether his offering was the small beginning of a great generosity.

Hello to the great generosity.

Whether it was a miracle of multiplication or a miracle of generosity is a matter for speculation. Either way, the people ate, and either way, they wished the Lord of the Hillside, the Lord of the Picnic, the Lord of Generosity to become their king. Small wonder. I'd have joined them in their desire. Their Picnic King had an eye for the little voice, and he understood that people were in need. Jesus seems to be aware of their desire to make him king, and he is made anxious by this desire. He escapes. He withdraws to the top of the mountain, and the people exit the narrative. The disciples, however, do not. They descend to the shoreline, and there descend into their boat, and there they wait. As they wait, a storm begins to brew, and the storm begins to come close. Still they wait. Eventually, as the storm comes even closer, they decide to move out into the water, to cross the lake while they can.

They meet the storm.

♀

Hello to the storm.

♀

I imagine that if the storm were serious enough to cause fishermen worry, then it must have been a dark storm that covered the lights of the night sky, a storm that blocked the light of the moon. Their boat would have been tipping and dipping and falling hither and thither. They were on the waters of chaos, and there was no light even by which to see the chaos. All they knew was their feeling, and their feeling was the unsteady wood beneath their feet: wood of a boat on an uncertain sea.

In the midst of this, they see something—or somebody—on the water coming toward them, and now they seem really afraid.

The voice calls to them, "It is I." But how could they even see what they couldn't see? And how could they keep their gazes straight when the surface upon which their boat floated was an uncertain and unruly stormy surface? It was Jesus walking on the waters that rocked them, walking where he shouldn't walk, being with them in the "here" of their fear.

The Gospel writer is a poet as well as many other things. Even though the disciples are in a rocking boat on a stormy sea, they make to take the water walker into the boat of uncertainty. As they begin to take him into their boat, they immediately reach the place that was their destination. It is as if to say that only in the middle of a storm can we find a truth that will steady us.

But we know that sometimes we search and search and search for what we cannot see, and still it stays dark and stormy.

Hello to the dark storm.

In this twin story is the story of a life. Sometimes it is stormy, and sometimes there is bread to share. Sometimes our picture of God is a food-sharing man on the side of a grass-covered hill; other times it's more frightening than we can imagine. We may prefer one story over another, but they both happen, over and over, again and again. While I am in the storm, someone else is on the hillside, and someone else is waiting in a boat, watching waves begin to form.

♀

The symbol for the Gospel of John in the Book of Kells is the Eagle. The eagle who can hover above and can descend quickly in a small movement. One time I invited a group to reflect on the images of the picnic and the sea of the Gospel of John, imagining the whole event happening all at once, and each of us an eagle, hovering above. Descending to the place that moves them, they are further invited to move into a part of the story, to describe it from the inside—the sights, the smells, the fears, the surprises.

One man said that he found himself walking with Jesus, distributing the bread from a little satchel that he found he had on his shoulders. His heart swelled with the love of the Lord of the Green Green Grass and the joy of feeding where there had previously been hunger. A woman said that she had been on the boat and had seen the Lord of Chaos walk across the waves. She now found herself at the shore giving words of calm to those waiting on the storm. "Don't worry," she said. "It's only a storm. Do what you need to do."

♀

A name is only shorthand for something much bigger. A collection of letters that will be pronounced, abbreviated, translated, and mispronounced. It's a metaphor for life. To name something is to begin a relationship with it. To name something is to abbreviate it into a short sequence of syllables, and if that naming is inadequate, it is a poor start.

When Merry and Pippin get lost in the forest in the second book of *The Lord of the Rings*, they find themselves in the company of a talking tree. They quickly share their names—both formal and abbreviated—and their kind. "Who calls you hobbits?" the Ent—for that is what he was—asks. "We call ourselves hobbits," they reply with an ease interpreted by the talking tree as hastiness. The Ent is both alarmed and amused at how quickly they tell him their names. However, he will not tell them his name: "For one thing it would take a long while: my name is growing all the time, and I've lived a very long, long time; so my name is like a story. Real names tell you the story of the things they belong to in my language, in the Old Entish as you might say. It is a lovely language, but it takes a very long time to say anything in it, because we do not say anything in it, unless it is worth taking a long time to say, and to listen to." To name something is part of the project of being human. The poet—or poets—who wrote the two stories of creation at the beginning of the first book of the Hebrew Bible understood that. God—who has many names—creates and names, creates and names, creates and names. When the first man—the Adam—is created, God invites him to give names to what is created, and this he does: "Whatever the Adam called every living creature, that was its name." The verb "to call" in Hebrew is *yiqra*. Like the English verb, it can mean many things—to summon, to proclaim, to be invited. To be named is to be summoned into being, and to name is to participate in this project of living.

Hello to the power of names.

I imagine that much of our desire to not name a place is because we fear that in naming it, we are giving it power, and by giving it power, we are saying that we may not escape. It's a valid fear. There are some suburbs of hell that we wish we'd never visited, and we neither want to give nor remember a name. And so, through energy, prayer, determination, or other hopes, we refuse to give a name to the place that we resent. To name something can be to call it into being, and we do not wish to call certain things into any kind of being.

Hello to this awful truth; it is here anyway.

In the biblical tradition, the writers are anxious about giving the name of God. To name something is to have power over it, and so God's name remains unknown. Chaos too is called many things—*pell-mell*, you could say, or *hither and thither*, or in Irish, *rí rá agus rúille búille*. Jesus of Nazareth met the chaos often in the form of a storm—and when he met it, he didn't name it, but he did use power over it. "Be quiet" is how his commands to the storm are often translated in our versions, but the Greek word is much stronger. The storm is like an angry dog or a demon, a force that cannot be put down, only contained. "Be muzzled" is what Jesus says. It is muzzled so it cannot bite. So we greet, and we muzzle.

Hello. Be muzzled.

♥

What is the name for the place where you now are? It requires close looking; it requires the dedication of observation and a commitment to truth. To name a place requires us to be in a place. It requires us to resist dreaming of where we should be and look around where we are.

Hello to here.

Hello to the name of here.

In the Shelter

How do we say hello to here?

There are many ways, but they all center on reality. They center on telling the truth to yourself and realizing the rotten fruit of illusion rarely fills for long. Once, I witnessed an argument between two men. It happened in a church meeting, a meeting in a church, a meeting with deep disagreement. I don't remember the details, but I do remember that the two men of God were yelling.

"I disagree with you," one yelled. "I am passionate, but not angry," he added, still yelling, by way of explanation.

"I am not angry either," the other yelled back.

This is a story about men, about religion, about anger, and about feeling. The men were removed from the truth and were using anger to deny the very anger they were denying.

I know too that this is a story about myself. Sometimes the story we tell about the place we are—even the place called anger—is a story that we try desperately to believe because the truth feels too hard to face.

An old boss of mine had a number of children, but his four-year-old daughter, Catherine, was my favorite. One time he said to her, "You've only got two emotions, Catherine, haven't you? You're either very happy or very sad."

She looked at him and said, "Or I'm very, very angry."

I took Catherine to weekday mass once. She sat on my shoulders and we walked to the church. At mass, she sat quietly, paying intense attention to everything. Afterward we went to get ice cream. "What did you think of mass?" I asked. "Boring," she said. She reached

22

up and touched the stubbled skin of my chin. "Why is your face so sharp?" she asked.

♀

When I moved to Australia, I took the opportunity to take the advice of a wise friend. She had said, "You're gay. You're a bit obsessed with religion. You'd better find someone to talk to." So I went to a psychotherapist.

Once, I described some small incidental detail to the psychotherapist. I must have described it vividly because he began laughing. When I finished, he said, "You tell a good story," and I looked at him and didn't understand what he meant. I was caught up in the drama of the story and the conundrum of how to resolve it. He was stopping along the way to admire the art. The story itself—and I forget the details—was a story about feeling mildly humiliated in front of somebody I wanted to impress. "Did you feel angry?" the psychotherapist asked me.

I remember my response well: "Oh, I don't get angry."

I know that this is not unusual. I know that many people, perhaps those affected—or is the word *infected*?—by religion, know these words particularly well. We try to be like God so we are slow to anger and overflowing in everlasting resentment.

The therapist said to me once, "Would you call yourself an angry man?"

I said, "I have problems with the word *anger* and problems with the word *man*."

23

I didn't want to call myself angry because that might summon anger, or proclaim or invite anger. It might be something final, and of all the things I didn't want to be, I most certainly didn't want to be truly angry. I didn't want to be called a man either, because I'd learned that gay men were failed men. But that didn't matter, because I was a man and I was angry, and I needed to stand in the here of anger and name things of power that were becoming more powerful because of my fear.

♦

"What do you want most in the world?" a friend asked me once.

"To be happy," I said without thinking, surprising myself with the truth. "How about you?"

"Oh, to be holy," he said.

"Shit," I thought, assuming I'd gotten it wrong again, assuming I was wrong again.

♦

A few years after I accidentally told the truth that I'd like to be happy, my dad gave me a book of poems for Christmas. It was an American textbook for undergraduate courses in poetry. He used the book as an excuse for what he called "a nice bookmark" and put some money in it.

In the textbook, I discovered a poem—"The Suitor" by Jane Kenyon:

Hello to here

> We lie back to back. Curtains
> lift and fall
> like the chest of someone sleeping.
> Wind moves the leaves of the box elder;
> they show their light undersides,
> turning all at once
> like a school of fish.
> Suddenly I understand that I am happy.
> For months this feeling
> has been coming closer, stopping
> for short visits, like a timid suitor.

Good writing, the adage tells us, is when we read something we've always known but never been able to put into words. I remember the moment when I read Jane Kenyon's poem. I understood the quiet approach of happiness. I understood that if happiness were to approach, it'd be wise to approach from the side, because I was likely to distrust anything too exuberant. It's perhaps an indication of my own temperament, as well as a story of Irish people. And—as I was discovering—a story of some American people too.

♀

Religion had rarely been something that gave me hope for happiness. Effort, certainly—I was used to reading religion as something that would inspire effort. From an early age, I had been introduced to guilt, while also learning love and generosity. So I was feeling more guilty, more burdened, and more exhausted than ever by Jesus, his Father, his holy Mother, and the Spirit. I was plagued with a fear that I was wrong, and for this no repentance was good enough.

What does it mean to believe that you are wrong? I don't mean that I was wrong about a fact. That would have been easy to correct. No, I was just wrong. Wrong, wrong, wrong. If you repeat a word often enough, it begins to sound strange. My trusted *Dictionary of Etymology* suggests that early forms of the word implied "twisted," "crooked," "wry" before evolving to imply "bad," "immoral," "unjust." Perhaps I'd have made a good Calvinist. But this haunting wasn't anything moral or religious. It wasn't a soul-turned impulse, it was a plague.

So to consider happiness was a fearful thing. Fortunately, I had religion. That'd fulfill the joint missions of keeping me miserable and Jesus glad.

However, there are always moments when goodness makes its own way to the center, despite our best efforts. If I ever saw somebody dance, I'd cry. Once, at a conference, I saw a dancer perform. She was so light on her feet, and the music so elegant, that I was mesmerized. I have never had the tools to nurture any real appreciation for modern dance, but I can still remember the craft of this woman's body, the hand that she extended to correspond with a note from a piano, the whimsy and extravagance in such an unnecessary act of beauty. Halfway through her piece, she moved from one side of the stage to the other, a distance of about twenty feet, and as she did it, she looked like music incarnated in a shaft of light. Her body spoke a truth of freedom and grace and movement and light.

Sometimes we are happy.

Hello to happiness.

♀

For a long time, I understood that religion was suspicious of happiness. Why would this be?

When I was twenty-five, I met a woman who was in her late fifties. She had recently been reading Henri Nouwen, she told me. She was talking about how moved she was by his words and how, having read many of his books, she realized she needed to start developing a theology of sorrow. I looked at her, aghast.

"How can you be your age and not already have a theology of sorrow?" I asked her.

Had she known me better, she might well have replied, "How can you be your age and not have a theology of joy?"

Hello to joy.

Hello to here.

♀

I have a habit that I sometimes practice and sometimes neglect, of twenty minutes of prayer in the morning time. It is often no more than staring at the little candle I've placed before an icon while I try to turn the heart and mind toward prayer, but sometimes it can unfold into a moment of surprise filled with the kindness and spaciousness of love. One particular time, I was surprised, but it was a fearful kind of surprise. I knelt to pray, and in the prayer, I was asking myself, "What is the way things are? What is happening now that I need to welcome?" I was so used to welcoming despair, or sorrow, or anxiety that I was shocked when I heard my deepest intuition answer that I was happy, and that happiness was what was here. It undid me. Happiness undid me.

I blew out the candle. I got up from kneeling and I walked out of the room. I did this with energy and purpose and strength and speed. All the while, I was observing my own self, my body, and wondering what the hostility toward happiness was.

Perhaps I was begging to be allowed to return to a Tomb that was so close to my name that I couldn't move from it. Perhaps I was so used to greeting sorrow that I viewed happiness with suspicion and doubt.

I had a friend years ago, Justin. He used to pray every day, and from time to time, I would see him sitting in the park, praying. Well, he said he was praying, but I always thought he looked constipated. "What happens when you pray?" I asked him once. "I sit and feel like shit for half an hour," he said, confirming my analysis. "And what happens then?" I asked. "I stop, and I feel better," he said. I suggested he might want to give up praying for a while. I took liberties and said that the God he prayed to might also prescribe this remedy. He laughed and said, "I wouldn't be able to get through a day without it." I felt for Justin because in him I could hear part of me.

The way I believed in God fed a distrust of life and a comfort with doom. Better the doomy god you know than the roomy god you don't, I suppose. A prayer attributed to St. Patrick, my namesake, speaks about how the life of Jesus effected the judgment of doom. I've recited that prayer since I was a child, but I never thought of what it could mean. I had judged doom, true, but I had judged it and deemed myself guilty. Justin and I were both in need of a little bit of judgment for our own little dooms, but we were too tied to the idea that God takes pleasure in burdening the burdened.

Hello to doom.

Hello to the judgment of doom.

With a bit of wisdom, a bit of age, and a bit of reading, my approach to happiness changed, the suspicion became hollow, and the embrace of gladness became less burdened. This was all helped by Ignatius of Loyola, a salty Basque soldier from the early 1500s who, because of an injury, had needed to rest for months. He read what was available to him—a commentary on the Gospels—and began to devise a way of prayer and living that has become known as the Spiritual Exercises, a pathway to prayer and telling the truth that has changed my life. I began a course of Ignatian spiritual direction when I lived in Australia, and there discovered

the words that were so important to Ignatius, words that he didn't
write but that transformed him:

~~The Glory of God is found in a human being fully alive.~~

○

I am suspicious of instant conversions, but it is inconveniently true
that ever since the day I read those words, my understanding of
God was reframed. Previously, I might have understood glory as
something shiny or sparkly. I might have thought of a fountain, or
a waterfall, or a shooting star, or phosphorescence. It was always
something without, something ungraspable, something inhuman. But
now, now, suddenly the glory of God was all around. I could perceive
it in the steadfastness of Peg, my eighty-six-year-old friend next to
whom I always sat at mass. I could see it in Blair when he danced,
in Elaine when she laughed, in Neil when he worked, in Craig when
he prayed, in Danielle when she asked questions and, suspicion of
suspicions, in myself when I landed on a word that I loved.

Tony Hoagland's poem "Grammar" is about a woman named
Maxine who has just returned from what sounds like a saucy weekend
with a guy named Phil. I know that I love this poem not only because
my brain tells me but also because my body tells me. I am unable to
not smile when I read it. In the poem, Maxine, so full of life, causes
heads to turn and bees move to her as if she is a flower of nurture:

> She is the one today among us
> most able to bear the idea of her own beauty,

Hello to here

and when we see it, what we do is natural:
we take our burned hands
out of our pockets,
and clap.

◉

Hello to glory.

◉

It has taken years to continue to live into the truth that if I believe
we are from God and for God, then we are from Goodness and for
Goodness. To greet sorrow today does not mean that sorrow will
be there tomorrow. Happiness comes too, and grief, and tiredness,
disappointment, surprise, and energy. Chaos and fulfillment will
be named as well as delight and despair. This is the truth of being
here, wherever here is today. It may not be permanent but it is here.
I will probably leave here, and I will probably return. To deny here
is to harrow the heart.

Hello to here.

Staring Match

I stare at the icon,
the sacrament, and
the sacred story.

I stare at the window,
the bread, and the
words.

I stare at the bruises too.
I repeat the questions
that infuriate me:

What was all this for? and:
What will all this bring? and:
What should I do now?

And then
there's that great silence
that greets me.

And I greet it, with
a liturgy of the morning,
a little vitamin of hate and

hope that opening the day with
rhythm might calm the
selves I ignore;

might help a life be lived
with generosity; might help the eye
worm inside the icon;

might help the story sound;
might help the bread be found;
by the some of me that's hungry.

2

Hello to the beginning

At a meal in London a few years ago, I was sitting with Noa, a deliciously salty woman from northern Israel. She combined her love for Torah with a love for truth and a love for story. I took an immediate liking to her. We were talking about religion—what else do you talk about?—and I asked her what she, as a Jew, makes of Christian interpretations of Hebrew texts, particularly those to do with literal seven-day creations, or abominations.

"Pah," she said.

Then she said the following, with no little theatricality: "We Jews don't ask the question about the first book of the Bible. We don't ask the question about the first chapter of the first book of the Bible. We don't ask the question about the first sentence of the first chapter of the first book of the Bible. We don't ask the question about the first word of the first sentence of the first chapter of the first book of the Bible. We ask why the first letter of the first word of the first sentence of the first chapter of the first book of the Bible is *B* when, according to religious poetic convention, it should be *A*."

Then she looked at me, wine-filled and happy, and said, "I like to think that it's a *B* because that letter in Hebrew looks a little like a picture of a house, and it's nice to think that at the beginning of Torah is an image of a home."

Noa was telling an old midrashic story in a new way. The midrash is an ancient commentary on the Hebrew texts: it asks questions of the story, it turns words upside down and puts both the word and the writer through tests and questions. One midrash is of a discussion between two rabbis who are speaking about the letter *A*.

Rabbi Jonah asks, "Why was the world created with (a word beginning with the letter) B?" and the answer came: "Just as [in Hebrew] the letter *B* is closed [at the back and sides] but open in front, so you have no right to expound what is above or below, before or afterward."

In the same midrash, the joyous argument continues: "For twenty-six generations the letter *A* made complaint before the Holy One, blessed be he, saying to him, 'Lord of the world! I am first among all the letters of the alphabet, yet you did not create your world starting with me!'"

The reply comes: "Said the Holy One, Blessed be he, to the A, 'The world and everything in it has been created only through the merit of the Torah. Tomorrow I am going to come and give my Torah at Sinai, and I shall begin (the Ten Commandments) only with you.'"

And so *A*, who was upset at being undone by the subordinate *B*, was satisfied to be the first letter of the Commandments, which, the letter *A* understood, existed before the world. And the story continues across other centuries.

Hello to the beginning

So, anyway, all of this is the long way around of saying that the beginning of things is important.

Hello to the beginning.

♀

Tá Dia láidir is máthair mhaith aige.
God is strong and has a good mother.

Irish proverb

I think that in order to understand the story of the body of Jesus, it's important to give long consideration to his mother. In Irish the name Mary is usually rendered as "Máire." However, when speaking of Mary the Mother of God, we do not call her "Máire." She—and she only—is known as "Muire." It's a sign of affection, a sign of honor, and a linguistic feature that I love.

My own mother met Mary once. She was bedded with grief following the death of her own mother. Ireland in the 1950s hadn't pretended to be kind, so it was through unkind years that my own mother had been mothered. Tough years, tough love. Tough times. Tough lives.

Hello to the tough.

And now my own mother's mother was dead. The afternoon that my mother met the Mother of God, the house was quiet. My mother, with her eight-times-stretched womb, was wrapped around its emptiness. She woke from an afternoon sleep to the sound of a woman coming into the room. The woman was in her seventies, dressed in tweed and soft clothes, gray hair. Iron gray, my mother said. She was like and unlike my mother's mother, and my mother knew her to be Mary, the Mother of God.

It's a tremendously intimate thing to have someone sit on the corner of your bed when you are remembering death. My mother describes the weight of the woman as she sat on the bed where she lay. She said that she felt the depression of the mattress. Those were her exact words.

The woman looked at my mother. She said, "You never liked me much, did you?"

My mother said, "No. You reminded me too much of someone else."

The woman with hair the color of iron said, "That's OK."

My mother heard a noise and turned and saw that my little brother had entered the room. She turned back and the woman was gone. The Mother of God. Mother of the Word Incarnate. The Star of the Sea. It didn't cause an earthquake of recovery; there was more time needed and rest, because grief is a tiring thing. But it was a little beginning.

♀

Oh, what is true?

Is it a good question to ask whether something happened or not? Is information recovery enough to mine this story for meaning? Is it true that the Blessed Virgin Mary visited my mother? Or is it true that it helped? If it's true that it helped, does it finally matter how it happened?

Hello to the beginning

There are libraries worth of books written on the origin of the Gospels. It's thought that Mark was the earliest, with the writers of both Matthew and Luke each using source material from Mark, as well as some independent sources of their own. I read a few scholars who suggested that the Gospel of Luke was written in Antioch, and suggesting that Mary the mother of Jesus went to Antioch, they hinted that perhaps Mary was the source of some of the stories of the birth of Jesus in Luke. It's a nice suggestion—although there are heavy shelves of books to counteract that idea.

Where would Mary learn courage? She had to learn it—a pregnancy with a dubious beginning and a family who wanted explanations. A confusing beginning to the life of a child—a long journey, a census, the birth in a place not her own. She would have been—I hope—surrounded by kinsfolk, women who knew the art and grief of birthing. But still, it was far from home, and anyway, the child was an unusual child. When she took him to the temple to be circumcised at eight days, an old man with the future in his eyes said that a sword would pierce her own soul.

The purpose of the Gospels is not live-action recall. It's not sequential impenetrability, even though they do sometimes seem impenetrable. Their purpose is rhetorical—to be realized and lived from, not just read. The measure of the reading is in the living.

Luke's Gospel opens as a letter, a kindness: "Since many have undertaken to set down an orderly account of the events that have been fulfilled among us, just as they were handed on to us by those who from the beginning were eyewitnesses and servants of the word, I too decided, after investigating everything carefully from the very first, to write an orderly account for you, most excellent Theophilus, so that you may know the truth concerning the things about which you have been instructed." The name Theophilus can mean "Lover of God," and scholars debate whether Theophilus existed or whether the name is a literary construct designed to embrace all who read this Gospel with care. It sets the scene—this text is written for those who love.

The text continues with politics then: "In the days of King Herod of Judea . . ." and we might imagine children's plays at Christmas with tea towel heads and blanketed shoulders, baby lambs and proud parents. But this is a story of older people, first, before it is a story of childhood. Zechariah and Elizabeth enter the scene, and both are righteous, but they have no children. Elizabeth, the mother of John, is an old woman who is faithful. But her womb is closed. In ancient literature, it is God who seals up the wombs of women. Control of the womb, in this literature, belongs neither to the women whose wombs are discussed nor to their husbands; it belongs neither to the community nor to whoever might grow in that womb. God is the one, as Phyllis Trible says, who opens wombs in judgment, blessing, and mystery.

To be forgotten is one thing. To be remembered with disgrace is another. One of the brothers in Taizé said that to be crucified is hard enough, but to keep living with a dying name is another kind of torture altogether. He was speaking of how religion is often populated with people whose names have suffered indignity. They may have been named a traitor, or like Elizabeth and her husband, they may have had things whispered about them because, while they were old and faithful, they were still childless and this was surely a judgment of a name. Their name would not continue, and so therefore their names were the subject of whispers, disgraceful whispers, whispers of disgrace.

Hello to disgrace.

Elizabeth's husband has been silenced by an angel, and it is a story of women—one considered too old to bear children and this other considered too unmarried to be pregnant—that ushers in this Gospel. But even more than this, it is a story both small and big. When John the Baptist was born, his father sang a song of his people, but earlier, when Elizabeth had realized she was pregnant, she was glad that the disgrace she had endured was taken away.

♀

Only in Luke's Gospel do we hear a story of Jesus, the boy of God. He was twelve and lost. His parents, who were returning from Jerusalem to their homeplace, thought he was with others, and it was a day before they realized he wasn't with them, then another day hurrying back to the city, and then three days before they found him. And when they found him, his answer was short. He asked them why they were searching for him, and he said, "Did you not know that I must be in my Father's house?"

One time, I was leading a discussion between some Christians and some Muslims on the subject of forgiveness in our sacred texts. The theologian David Tombs was in the group and he pointed to this text, saying that, as a parent of children, were he to hear a response like this, he'd be in need of forgiving them for their answer, never mind their absence. Therefore, he made a theological conclusion that to be in the position of needing to forgive God who is so easily lost is to be in a position of faithfulness. Hearing that fine formulation, I breathed easier.

I wonder too if the Gospel writer also was uneasy with this story. This story of the lost boy of God finishes with "And Jesus increased in wisdom and in years." To increase in years is a simple matter of getting older. But to increase in wisdom is a matter of growing up. And that isn't always as simple.

Avivah Zornberg says that when we read the stories of Adam and Eve in the garden, we are tempted to read them as not human. Who are these parentless creatures walking in a holy garden with God? They are far from us. However, when they hide, when they are ashamed, when Adam blames the woman for exposing him to unholy eating, then, then, then we recognize. "Ah," we say, "now I see humanity."

Part of the difficulty in reckoning with the character of Jesus is that he has the problem of perfection. The Christian faith praises him as sinless. The Catholic understanding of Mary declares that she was born as a result of an immaculate conception—she herself was free from the bruise of original sin. The topic is wider than a paragraph and has limitations and possibilities, but one of its problems is that it seems to remove both Jesus and his strong mother from the effects of being ordinary. We can ask about when he fell, or when he cried, or when he had nightmares. But we must also ask when he learned truth, or courage, or integrity. When did he learn the human art of apology? How did he live with his own body, the move from boy to man, the richness of a life lived in tension?

Hello to the beginning

So what do we do with the perfectly parented incarnation of God? Do we read his life and hear our own selves, or do we read his life and feel like he was the light of God covered by skin? Did he ever break? For many Christians, it is imperative to understand that Jesus was sinless, but this can make him also seem inhuman, because we know ourselves by our limitations. When Jesus rose, he showed his disciples some of his scars. Some people say that his scars were the way in which he atoned for humanity's failures. But it's also good to read it as the wounds of his own life, the marks of survival, etched into his own skin.

Hello to the things that teach us how to be human.

●

"I believe good poets borrow, great poets steal," wrote Meg Kearney in her poem "Creed." She's right. And she'd know, too, because she stole the line from T. S. Eliot, who said that "one of the surest of tests is the way in which a poet borrows. Immature poets imitate; mature poets steal." There again, he was also stealing, in a way, but he was stealing and turning, because W. H. Davenport Adams wrote an article in *The Gentleman's Magazine* in 1892 saying that "great poets imitate and improve, whereas small ones steal and spoil."

The writer of the Gospel of John stole lines for the beginning of his text. In the beginning, he starts, and he starts with a steal, because he's started with the words about the beginning from the story that begins with a *B*.

For years, I have worked with groups and have asked them the following question: "If, right now, you were to write the story of your life, what would the first sentence be?" The responses are engaging. Recently, one man who had suffered a bereavement said, "In the beginning we were four; just after the beginning, we were three." He took the first three words of Genesis and then told his own story. He used numbers to add up to the number of days described in Genesis: four and three make seven, after all. But his first sentence told a story of subtraction, not addition. Four minus one means you're three plus grief.

Hello to things that don't add up.

In a room in England, a woman once said, in answer to the question about the first sentence of the story of your life, "Once upon a time, in the beginning, I heard a story." She was mixing faith with fairy tale, and she told a magnificent story.

ϙ

Elizabeth Bowen said that "to have turned away from everything to one face is to find oneself face to face with everything." The poet Christian Wiman quotes this when speaking about falling in love. It can also speak wisdom to the incarnation. Christianity hopes that God turned toward each life in the body of a child, and Christians hope that we turn toward God in turning toward Jesus of Nazareth. And in so doing, we each turn toward each other.

Maybe the Shakers were right. Maybe it's only by turning and turning that we'll come round right. A small religious group, they branched off from the Quakers in eighteenth-century England. Many moved to America, and there they met in small white wooden places of worship, where they sang, danced, and turned. They have a hymn, "Simple Gifts," written by Elder Joseph Brackett:

> 'Tis the gift to be simple, 'tis the gift to be free
> 'Tis the gift to come down where we ought to be,
>
> And when we find ourselves in the place just right,
> 'Twill be in the valley of love and delight.
>
> When true simplicity is gained,
> To bow and to bend we shan't be ashamed,
>
> To turn, turn will be our delight,
> Till by turning, turning we come 'round right.

John's Gospel doesn't mention the birth of Jesus, and it doesn't mention much about his family. In this Gospel, thought to be the last written Gospel, Jesus calls his mother "woman," and people call Jesus the son of Joseph from Nazareth. The Gospel opens up with a poem praising the Word and the beginning, praising light, light that shines in darkness. The main themes of the Gospel are set out: life and death, belief and unbelief, acceptance and rejection in the world, humanity and God, flesh and glory, seeing and not-seeing. It's like a film that starts with a dream—the opening sequence only makes sense once you've seen it all. The idea is to return and return and re-turn, turning like the Shakers in a never-ending turn of repentance toward the life who is the light of all the world.

The writer of the Gospel doesn't stop stealing after the first few words, however. He began with the beginning, and then there was the dream poem and an introduction to John the Baptist. Then, nonchalantly, the narrator continues: "The next day . . ."

It is the poverty of regularity that the surprise of these words doesn't strike us. The Gospel of John has begun with an epic poem describing light and glory and darkness and power and then, suddenly, the writer has simply written, "The next day . . ." Three times at the end of the first chapter of his Gospel, the writer writes, "The next day," and then the second chapter opens with "Three days later." The days are progressing, and so is the stealing. The writer of John began by stealing words about the beginning, but now he is stealing words about seven days, and in the first story, there was rest on the seventh day. In John's story, on the day of rest, there is a wedding, and at the wedding there is a shortage of wine. Did Jesus dance? How could he not? The wine was found, but only after a person who is called "Woman" presses Jesus toward action. Mary, Woman, the second Eve, is urging the flesh of her flesh to do something that he seems reluctant to do.

The writer of John's Gospel is a poet telling us something about how he reads the beginning of the world. He believes in the power of words, and he believes that words have power and that words come from a Word that was at the beginning. All we are short of is the garden. But John waits until the end before mentioning the garden.

Hello to the beginning

John's Gospel doesn't mention the birth of Jesus. Instead, it places him as the birth of the world. But I have a lot of time for the Dublin poet Paul Durcan, who commenting on the readings at mass one Sunday in 1985, said,

> It's a long way from a tin of steak-and-kidney pie
> For Sunday lunch in a Dublin bedsit
> To cedar trees in Israel.

What difference can the life of a man born into a noble culture two thousand years ago make to us today? If he had been born in South America, would we be celebrating liturgies by drinking maté and chewing coca leaves? If he'd been born in Ireland, would we drink whiskey and break brown soda bread? The Irish word for "whiskey" is *uisce beatha*, translating literally as "water of life." God may have been on to a good thing had the incarnation been on my turf.

If the incarnation means anything, it must speak to us on our own turf. It must enter into the clay of our landscapes, the texture of our languages, and the tensions of our cultures. In the introduction to *The Anchor Book of New American Short Stories*, Ben Marcus wrote that there are only two types of story: a person went on a journey and a stranger came to town. In a way, one can understand the Gospels as both of those stories. A god went on a journey toward the gardens of the city, and a stranger came to town in the body of a Galilean.

Hello to the story of beginnings.

So much of the life of Jesus is summed up in the cross—the image of the cross is seen so often, as fashion, as religion, as politics, as patriotism. There are crosses with Jesus on it and crosses with Jesus off it. And yet while many argue that the cross was the most important aspect of his life, it cannot be understood without understanding the richness of his whole life. Who taught him to read? Who made his clothes? Who were his friends? What made him cry?

What were his first words?

It is a pity that the image of the Madonna and Child is seen as a denominational image—mostly only loved and displayed by the liturgical traditions. The way I see it, this image of a woman with a baby is the image of incarnation and an image for all people who approach the faith of the incarnation. It says "flesh of my flesh," and it says that body and blood and sinew and sweat became holy in a story and became wholly us. Irenaeus of Lyons is credited with saying, "What was not assumed was not redeemed"—he was arguing against those who saw Jesus as a puppet strung with God's strings, not really human, just pretending, light covered in a thin layer of skin. To appreciate the death of this Jewish stranger, we must appreciate the bones of this man.

It is not unholy to ask about his ignorance. If he had to learn, then it meant that he was limited, and his limitations were not antithetical to his life, identity, and goodness. When studying theology, I tried to memorize theological equations using words like the hypostatic union discussing Jesus's dual nature as both God and Human, and I heard philosophical lectures about whether, on the cross, it was both of the natures of Jesus that died, or only one. I can't remember the opinions—I've always been much more interested in poetry than mathematics—but what I do remember is that in order to understand the death of Jesus, we must understand the birth of Jesus, the life of Jesus, the friendships of Jesus, and the tensions of Jesus.

○

Recently, in England, I gave a group that task about imagining the first line of the story of their lives. One woman, sitting near me, wrote that she was in her eighties now, and she had loved how wild life had been. To my ear, she had placed special emphasis on the word "wild" when she read her line aloud, so I asked her about it and she said, "Oh, I forgot. Wild and precious is what I meant to say. Wild and precious."

The Gospel of Matthew begins with a long genealogy. The Greek word for "genealogy" is *genesis*. So, in a way, Matthew's Gospel too goes back to the beginning, although not as far as the beginning with the Word. He begins with Abraham and then details three lists of fourteen. The writer notes that there were fourteen generations from Abraham to David, fourteen generations from David to the Babylonian Exile, and then, following the Exile, fourteen generations from the Exile to the Christ. It's a neat theological family tree, and the structure itself tells a story. Three generations of fourteen is akin to six counts of seven, with Jesus being the last of the sixth and the first of the seventh. The Hebrew tradition has a long relationship with certain numbers—there were seven days described in the beginning and there were twelve tribes who spent forty years in the desert. The Hebrew tradition isn't alone in ascribing power to certain numbers. Ireland has a long tradition of honoring the seventh son of the seventh son. "He has healing," my mother said to me about a man who was coming to our village. "What?" I asked. "He has healing," she repeated. "He's the seventh son of the seventh son." I wondered what powers the seventh daughter of the seventh daughter had, and I didn't bother going to the man's public meeting.

♥

In Jane Austen's *Pride and Prejudice*, a great noblewoman has heard that her noble nephew, Mr. Darcy, may soon become engaged to a woman of inferior birth. So when the noblewoman—Lady Catherine de Bourgh—speaks to the woman of inferior birth, Elizabeth Bennet, she mentions the honor of her own maternal line and condescends to describe the "respectable honorable and ancient, though untitled, families" of her paternal genesis. Lady Catherine objects to Elizabeth, a woman without "family, connections or fortune," marrying a member of her own family, seeing that such a connection would "disgrace him in the eyes of everybody."

Matthew's genealogy tells us of dubious connections and stories hidden within wild stories. Abraham was the father of Isaac, but everybody knows that Abraham thought that killing Isaac would be a demonstration of faithfulness and Isaac never saw his father after that awful day, preferring to go to the wilderness where Hagar had fled. Then Judah was the father of Perez, but Perez was the younger of twins, and their mother had once been Judah's daughter-in-law before she became his wife. Rahab was a wise woman who knew defeat when she saw it, and so she navigated a way out of death by negotiating with soldiers from an unwelcome army, and Ruth was a Moabitess, a lineage despised for their origins and characteristics. Even David himself was a shepherd lad, ill considered as a potential king, and the first and second book of Kings isn't so sure how to tell the story of this warrior musician, so it tells it multiple times, with different threads. David, though, after he had made a name for himself through success in battle, stayed about the home and demanded Bathsheba's body and, ultimately, once it became clear that Bathsheba was pregnant, the life of her husband.

Hello to the book of bruised generations.

♀

In many ways it may be that we are moving beyond the times when whisperings of lowly circumstance are anything beyond enjoyable information. But—I know this to be true—there are new ways that families are shamed by secrets that shouldn't have to be kept. I know a man who once lived in the body of a woman. His family left him, and so he learns about relatives' deaths in the newspaper and learns about nephews and nieces through secret letters sent from a sympathetic cousin.

This is the truth. He has nothing to be ashamed of. The secret of the secret is that it is the family's shame, not his shame, that is to be exposed.

Hello to the secret of secrets.

The genealogy of Matthew's Gospel honors the wild and precious lives of the old family of Jesus. To honor the lives lived—especially those lives that, while lived, were hated—is a testimony to truth and an undermining of the capacity of shame and scapegoating. It is convenient, particularly convenient, to tell stories of the past lives—especially our own past lives—that create a strong distinction between good and evil. The genealogy of Matthew's Gospel shows us that what may have once been considered scandalous is, with the greater wisdom of hindsight, demonstrated to have been motivated by courage.

Andrew Solomon, in his book *Far from the Tree*, writes that "love is not only an intuition but also a skill." Courage may be the same: it abides within us, alongside the landscape of fear, and it is by practicing courage that courage grows. The practice of courage is needed most in situations where it is most threatened, and it is often those who have the most to lose who are the ones from whom the most courage is needed.

📍

Samuel Johnson said that "courage is the greatest of all virtues, because if you haven't courage, you may not have an opportunity to use any of the others." Maya Angelou has echoed this by saying that "courage is the most important of all the virtues, because without courage you can't practice any other virtue consistently. You can practice any virtue erratically, but nothing consistently without courage." In American Sign Language, the sign for courage implies strength that comes from the body, with both finger-spread hands beginning at the chest and moving out to form the letter "s" for strength. The sign is similar in British Sign Language. What is it about courage that has to come from within? And where within does it come from? What is interesting is that the sign for "fear" in British Sign Language uses the same finger-spread hand and touches the chest. It is as if to imply that the difference between fear and courage is whether what is in you comes to the fore or not. It occurs to me that courage comes from the same place as fear, and where there is fear, there is the possibility of courage.

●

The Gospel of Matthew begins with a family tree of characters, characters whose lives were shaped by chance, circumstance, and courage. The Christian story of incarnation in the body of a boy—a boy whose ancestors were both famous and infamous—is one that can spur us toward living with the courage that is indigenous to us. To be human is to be in the image of something good, and image comes from imagination. To be human is to be in the imagination of God, and the imagination is the source of integrity as well as cracks. To be born is to be born into a story of possibility, a story of failure, a story of imagination and the failure of imagination. To be born is to be born with the possibility of courage.

Hello to courage.

In the Shelter

What does courage feel like? I remember, at a charismatic prayer meeting, somebody asked a different question that has a similar answer. The question asked was "How do you know if God is speaking to you?" The answer given was "It has all the signs of a minor heart attack." At the time I found it mostly funny, now I find it fairly problematic, but still I am struck by the wisdom of recognizing the body. When we are in a moment of courage—whether we call that God's voice or indigenous bravery—it is the body that tells us a deep truth; it is the body that speaks to us, and it is from the body that the courage comes.

I have a friend, Kellie, and when she speaks courageously—and she speaks courageously often—you can read the truth from her body. Her fingers shake a little bit, and her mouth, while it is shaping strong words, is also shaking with the fear that demonstrates the depth of her courage.

Hello to fear.

Hello to the courage that comes from the same place as fear.

Hello to the truth of the body.

The Irish language is replete with sayings about language and its relationship to landscape and culture.

Ní tír gan teanga, we learned as children—"There is no nation without a language." And also the same thing in a different way,

Tír gan teanga, tír gan anam—"A land without a language is a land without a soul." In a show of rhyming nationalism, the phrase *Is fear gaeilge briste ná béarla cliste* was rattled like a tongue twister by our class—"Broken Irish is better than Clear English." My favorite, however, is *Beatha teanga í a labhairt*—"The life of a language is in its speaking."

To speak or—better still—to communicate is a marker of most animals. We communicate with the body, we communicate with sound, and we communicate through something ungraspable that causes lines of connection—whether of fear or love—between us and others.

◉

Here's a question:

When did God first cry? Or—in another way—
When did God first realize the limitations of language?

◉

Mark's Gospel pays no attention to birth narratives of Jesus. Mark's Gospel is understood to be the earliest, and it is the Gospel with the least attention to Jesus's sermons and an absolute discrimination in favor of action over sentiment. The writer of this earliest Gospel begins bluntly: "The beginning of the good news of Jesus Christ, the Son of God," except here "beginning" is *archē* in Greek, from where we get the English word "archetype."

This Gospel, paying such attention to action, has within it a story of archetype that, truthfully, was another conversion for me.

In the story, there is a man who lives among the tombs. All day long he howls and gashes himself with rocks. He is restrained, from time to time, by chains, but he breaks those chains. The story doesn't state who his chainmasters were, but that's part of the story. He is a small image of living death. He is barely in his own body—it is almost as if his gashing of himself is an attempt to exit his body—and yet he is entirely within the protest of his own body. He is alive, but he lives in the places of death.

Jesus of Nazareth, fresh from muzzling a stormy sea, lands on the shore where this man is living. It is strange that the story associates the shoreline with tombs. When I die, I would like to be buried where the land meets the sea, but this shoreline was not a pleasant place, it seems, certainly for this anonymous man. Jesus lands and has begun interacting with this as-yet-anonymous man, and the man protests. In a small twist of irony, the man begs Jesus, by God, not to hunt his demons from him. Jesus asks him what his name is. The man answers, "My name is Legion, for we are many."

This can be read in so many ways. The word *legion* is a militaristic word, and the Roman legion that had decamped to this particular geographic area bore the boar as their standard on their banners. This answer of the anonymous man can also be understood simply, and powerfully, as an indication of the dignity of language.

"What is your name?" he was asked. And he answered, "I am what has afflicted me." How many of us know the truth of this? When we are toward the end of ourselves, we begin to believe that we are only what we struggle with. The man here tells us a truth that is awful—we baptize ourselves with names that are far from the only truth about ourselves.

My name is Legion, for we are many. He reminds me of Gollum, who, in Peter Jackson's depiction of Tolkien's work, says, "They cursed us, and drove us away. And we wept, Precious, we wept to be so alone. And we only wish to catch fish so juicy sweet. And we forgot the taste of bread, the sound of trees, the softness of the wind. We even forgot our own name."

The primary impulse of God in the first story of beginning is seen in naming, and it is a project shared with the Adam in the second story of beginning. This man has begun to believe the diabolical about his name.

♀

My youngest sister, Méabh, is, like Maxine in Tony Hoagland's poem, filled with the joy of being alive. When she was younger, I remember my father telling the older siblings not to mention to Méabh the fact that her namesake in Irish mythology was the bloodthirsty Queen of Connaught. She was the enemy of her former husband, and when a druid told her that one of her sons would kill her former husband and that this killing son would be called Maine, she named all seven of her sons Maine. Queen Méabh demanded equal wealth with her new husband, and she was killed by the son of an enemy. My father was worried that Méabh's sunny disposition would be darkened by learning the story of her warmongering namesake.

We should have known better. When she found out, she—all thirty-six months of her—cackled with delight and requisitioned wool blankets and cereal boxes as cloaks and crowns in her games of Warrior Queens of Ireland.

Hello to our name.

Hello to the names we call ourselves.

📍

The story of the man who calls himself Legion continues, and the affliction in the man speaks, begging Jesus to be sent to the nearby swine. Scholars suggest that the understanding of the time may have been that demons, in order to leave their host, needed to find another sentient host; if they are sent into the air, they will kill their final host. It's only an opinion, and the drama of the story continues. Jesus allows the demons to go from the man to the swine, and the whole herd of swine—two thousand of them—charge from the cliffside into the sea, bringing death from land to water. There are many questions to be asked—not least about the owners of the pigs—but one of the things that I think is most moving is that the man who hitherto had held such chaos within him was now seeing his chaos externalized. He had survived with all that destruction within him.

Hello to the things that we survive, for they are many.

The people from the town near the tombs near the sea came to see what had happened, and when they did come, they saw the man—the text is careful to name him as "the very man who had had the legion"—clothed and in his right mind. That he is now clothed implies that he had previously been unclothed. He was unpersoned in his name and unclothed in his body, more than human and less than human all at once. The people see the man in his own mind, and they are afraid and they beg Jesus to leave.

James Alison is a theologian from England who has written many books, but I will always be glad for the first book of his I read, and a particular chapter in that book: "Clothed and in His Right Mind." Echoing René Girard, James Alison asks the question "Why would the people be afraid?" and to answer it he returns to the question of chains. Who chained the man up? Was he chained up because he was howling all night and day, gashing himself with stones and breaking chains? Or was he howling all night and day, gashing himself with stones and breaking chains because he was chained up? It must be a fearful thing to see the zombie by whose name you threaten children in his own mind. It is the story of the scapegoat come to tea, and the scapegoat knows more about your wishes than you'd wish, for we are willing to show aggression toward those from whom we fear the least revenge. The clothed man was not necessarily on a pathway of revenge, but the awful lesson awaiting him was that his very being, his very incarnation in his own body and mind, was itself a threat of revenge toward those who may have kept him chained up.

He, like so many other characters in this story, begs Jesus for something. The demons had begged and their begging was granted. The people, upon seeing the unmanned man made man again, begged Jesus to go, and Jesus did go. The man himself, seeing fear, begged Jesus to take him with him, but this most reasonable of requests was denied. Jesus tells him to go home to his *sos*, his family, friends, and kin. But who are they? The demons? The pigs? The skeletons of his tombhome?

Jesus was, in effect, asking the man to live with courage, to treat those who had treated him as an animal with a dignity of humanity. It must have taken generosity, imagination, and bravery. There was another cave. This cave was wider—it was the wide world. He was asked to live fully in the life of the community. The cave was not a hiding place. The cave was a sending place.

Hello to the wide, wide world.

♀

As a gay man walking carefully through the halls of God, I had got used to the names that were used about me and had even begun to adopt some of them for me. During some complicated days when I was enduring exorcisms for the demon of homosexuality, the text about this unnamed man was quoted as a justification for all kinds of horrors. I was told that if I called myself gay, it was like this man calling himself Legion; he was not legion, and I was not gay. But my sexuality wasn't demonic; the words being used about my sexuality were. As I began to find language of my own, I also stumbled into using language that would keep me bound by the very indignities that had initially bound me. I saw myself as a victim of theologies: theologies that hated me. From the edges, though, I heard words from a strange unnamed man, a man from a region called the Gerasenes. He said, do not leave the people who caused you so much pain. It may be that in owning your own name, you too can be a possibility of giving them a new name—the name of friends, the name of family, the name of kin.

> *Beatha teanga í a labhairt.*
> The life of a language is in its speaking.
> Hello to the story of people who learn their names.
> Hello to speaking your own name.

Day of the Dead

After the priest said
You shouldn't be here at
this time of day,

I looked at his face
for any trace
of shame

at chasing the
desperate
from the raw regions
of prayer.

And I said
What is your name?

And he said
I am legion.
And I said

Are you one or many?
And he said
Yes. He said

Place your bets on this—
You do not belong.
You will not belong.

It will not be long
before you long
for anonymity.

I gathered my
belongings
and left the place of prayer

thinking
I shouldn't have gone there
in the first place,

thinking
there was no-one there
with a kind face,

thinking:
there was no-one there.

3

Hello to the imagination

The history of religion in its widest sense (including therefore mythology, folklore, and primitive psychology) is a
treasure-house of archetypal forms from which the doctor
can draw helpful parallels and enlightening comparisons for
the purpose of calming and clarifying a consciousness that is
all at sea. It is absolutely necessary to supply these fantastic
images that rise up so strange and threatening before the
mind's eye with some kind of context so as to make them
more intelligible. Experience has shown that the best way to
do this is by means of comparative mythological material.

Carl Jung

Having been haunted by caves since my childhood, I found real
solace in the spirituality of Ignatius of Loyola. He recommended
using the imagination for prayer and would encourage individuals
to picture the landscape of their internal life—whether that's a field,
a cave, a storm, or a bird.

Experiences in charismatic Christianity also helped in this—because often there is much space given to the intuitive in these contexts. "I have a picture," somebody might say in the middle of a prayer time, "and it's of a group of people all dressed in gray, but one of them is wearing pink boots." The more I learned about Ignatius and the more I experienced psychotherapy, the more I began to trust these images, not as Polaroids fresh from Jesus, but as yearnings of the intuition.

Hello to a picture of truth.

Under the guidance of Ignatius of Loyola and a spiritual director, I began to use imagery for prayer—sometimes furnishing rooms or locking doors with a force that surprised me. Jung's understanding of imaginative symbol too helped assert an independence and dignity in engaging with characters rising from the unconscious. All of this reasonably self-focused work helped, in a delightful way, when I found myself in need of a job.

I got a job as a chaplain at the De La Salle Pastoral Centre in West Belfast, a center that provides daylong religious retreats for schools—in practice it is mostly Catholic schools that send their pupils there, but they are open to all schools. Margaret, my boss for that rich year, said to me on my first day that I had three aspects to my job. First, every young person who came through the door should be called by their own name, and I should use whatever method I wanted, but I needed to speak to the person using their own name. Second, they should have a positive experience in speaking about faith—whether they loved or hated faith, their experience of speaking about it should be positive. Finally, all groups of young people should have the opportunity to deepen friendships with each other as part of their retreat. It was, without doubt, the best job description I'd ever had, and one to live up to.

New batches of students came to the center every day. They usually came in class groups of between twenty and thirty people. The day itself was reasonably unsurprising in its timetable; there were some games, opportunities to talk about school or music, opportunities to talk about faith and to talk about what's important, time for relaxation and sport, and a prayer service at the end of the day, a prayer service that the young people themselves would design. Part of the day was to have an experience of prayer, and so I fell back on Ignatius and image and the imagination.

When we would have a prayer time, I would remove all the chairs from the room and place cushions on the floor, circled around what Margaret liked to call a *focus*, a small makeshift altar of holy things. I had a beautiful piece of cloth from Ethiopia, a prayer bowl, a few candles, and icons from different parts of the world. Young people could put anything they wanted into that space too. We'd talk about what was there and talk about our upcoming prayer time.

The prayer time itself was simple. Each person was invited to close their eyes and to imagine themselves taking a walk. This walk, they were invited to imagine, was in a pleasant place of their own choosing, at a time of their own choosing. They were feeling content and were asked to imagine the scenery. At one point, they see a stranger coming toward them, and on closer inspection, they realize it is Jesus. He greets them by their own name—and here I'd say the name of everyone in the room—and they engage in a conversation.

Depending on the age of the group, the conversation was different, and as time went by I gave fewer specifics and left more room for them to engage with the words of their own choosing. After a while they were also told that if they wished to say anything at all to this character, they could—and then to listen for a response. Shortly after that, the imagination exercise came to an end with them saying goodbye in whatever way they wanted. The whole process took only four or five minutes, and then for the rest of the session, we talked about the imagination and the images seen.

I found a book by Mary Terese Donze, *In My Heart Room*, as helpful as it was simple. Following her practice, I began opening the session by leading everybody in three deep breaths and then using the same simple way to close the session. Technically, there are some ways in which oxygen-rich blood can help relaxation and focus, but mostly I did it to help people open and close an exercise of the imagination with calm and clarity—in particular, it was to help anybody who was feeling nervous about opening their eyes as the exercise ended.

Any group of people will be prone to the self-consciousness that can accompany such group experiences—"What will people say?" "Will I be laughed at?" Much of what I considered my job was to contain the space of reflection in a way that focused things away from teasing and more on respecting the time. The groups were told that it'd take about five minutes and that if they were bored, well, that was entirely understandable, but to make sure to be bored quietly so as not to interrupt anybody else who was wishing to use their imagination. To my surprise, this invitation worked, and it was very rare that anybody said anything that indicated even a hint of bullying. As we discussed, each person was asked questions, but they were told that there was an easy way to shut the Corkman up—to say, "I'll keep my thoughts to myself." Regularly a person would use this line—whether because they wanted to keep something to themselves or to test the integrity of my promise—and it was my job to accept this easily and without drawing any more attention to the individual than they'd want.

These weren't angels either. They were ordinary young people, mostly from Belfast. They used colorful language, demonstrated that their imaginations were uncolonized by religious rhetoric, and spoke freely and easily. They spoke of the Jesus of their imagination with clarity and insight, and they spoke of their own inner lives with integrity and courage.

I loved this job more than I have ever loved any other job.

♀

I always imagined myself walking in woods near the shore when I was in these prayer exercises. But the places that young people put themselves were entirely varied. One said, "I was walking first in a park and then I was by my wee cousin's grave." Others saw themselves at a beach, or in the woods, or in a favorite place—a holiday venue or the street near their grandparents' house.

Their experiences of Jesus were intriguing. Each day was a new experience for me, and as time went by I tried to learn lines of introducing a suggestion easily and simply and with the least amount of words possible. This was a time for space and ease, not for invasive instruction.

One young person said, "Jesus and I went to feed the ducks," and many of them described Jesus's clothes. They went from the unsurprising—he was a man in robes with brown hair—to the utterly surprising. One young person said, "Pádraig, I was bored during the talk, so I used my own imagination to go where I wanted. I decided to take a walk on the sea, and as I was walking, climbing over waves, I noticed Jesus coming toward me. He was in a purple tutu and wearing a coconut bra." Often the groups would draw pictures of their experiences on a group poster that would be brought back for their teachers. This young child who'd met Jesus in a coconut bra said to me, "I'm not very good at drawing, so I think I'll just color in shapes." I was mostly relieved and mildly disappointed.

It was, without doubt, an honor to be treated to the experiences of the inner life of the retreat participants. They spoke with ease about the things that they brought to prayer—questions about their friendships, schools, and future careers, questions about death, and curiosity about growing up.

One eleven-year-old said, "I asked Jesus what I'd be when I grow up and he said, 'I don't know—it depends on what you want.'" The nonchalance with which the Jesus of this young person's imagination said "I don't know" moved me. There was an interest, but not a controlling or guiding interest, in the reply. One child who was finishing primary school and hoping desperately to get into a particular secondary school said, "I told him about the school that I want to get into, and he said, 'Oh, I know somebody else who went there.'" This Jesus was as casual in conversation as the young person was concerned about changes in life. In that same class, a child said, "I told Jesus I was worried I wouldn't fit into my new school, and he said, 'Well, everyone's different.'"

This person of their imagination was neither shocked nor overly dramatic in his replies. They were easy, calm, and usually a rich voice of containment. One young person told me how they responded to a question from Jesus: "'What are you looking forward to about secondary school?' Jesus asked me. 'Armpit hair,' I told him." I, together with everybody else, enjoyed the laugh that had clearly been at the heart of this small story from a brave young person. I also found myself remembering my own wonder and shock of a changing body, and I admired this voice of courage to name the waited-for change. Another responded to a different question that came from Jesus: "I told him I wanted to be a footballer, and he said, 'What if you don't get that?' and then I said a lawyer." There was a wisdom that was far from certitude in these imaginations.

Hello to growing up.

It was inevitable that death would enter the room in these conversations, and I had to remind myself to respond to stories and curiosities about death with ease and without drama. "I asked Jesus to say hello to everybody I know up in heaven," one child said, "and he said he would and that they are all having a nice time." Another said, "I asked him why my grandpa had to die. He said, 'There was a lot wrong with him.'" I was struck by the concrete reality of these responses from the Jesus of their imagination. My guess is that the best of their parents', friends', and their own wisdom was projected into these experiences, and I was moved to hear the stories and the concrete reality of the Jesus of their imagination.

Hello to death.

On the walk, many described their surroundings. One child said, "I saw somebody lonely and Jesus sent a dog to them for company," and another told me, "I was walking along a path, and the path was surrounded on both sides by snow. Everywhere, built on the snow, were igloos. Igloos here and igloos there. Jesus came toward me, wearing a tuxedo and sipping a martini. I asked him what the real meaning of life was, and he gave me an answer that was both confusing and satisfactory." Needless to say, somebody asked him what the answer had been, and he said, "I'll keep it to myself." He was a genius at storytelling.

Another said, "Jesus saw a lonely baby and he carried it with him. He made the baby's eyes light up," and clearly reflecting on Sunday readings of the feeding of the five thousand, one student asked, "Sir, can Jesus just, like, pop out a pizza whenever he wants?"

The integrity of the imagination reflected other truths about religion and life too. One young person said that for the first while after Jesus came to her, there was an awkward silence. I asked her how she felt about it, and she shrugged and said, "It was all right." To imagine the embodiment of God being caught in a moment of awkward silence and to hold that as easily as this pupil did was, in my estimation, a remarkable feat of theological containment.

Hello to the imagination

Another young person said, "I was walking on the surface of the sun, and it was very hot. Jesus came along in a thick bubble so that he wasn't being burned." The imagination continued to incorporate spaceships and stars and an exploding sun. It was vivid, and apocalyptic, and it struck me that this young person would find company in a number of the authors of apocalyptic material in both the Hebrew and Christian texts. The Jesus of her imagination was behind a thick bubble that protected him from what burned others, and I thought of how truthfully she was reflecting a religious culture that often patronizes rather than respects young people.

Hello to the truths we don't want to hear.

♥

A question I was always curious to ask was "What was Jesus like?" The answers were often given in the context of reciprocality—he was nice because this is how I felt. Practical theology describes how intention and effect must be mutually revealing of each other. That which is called good must cause good; otherwise goodness is to be queried.

One student said, "When we were talking, it felt nice to be listened to. My mum and dad love me and all, but they are often very busy doing all the things for me, and when I talk to anyone, there's so much noise. So it was nice to be listened to." The insight into this—the distinction between busy love and listening love—was well made. Here was a critique from a girl who was little more than twelve years old, who understood her own needs well and also understood what it felt like to be tired. Another student said, "When

Jesus knew my name, it felt normal. When I could say anything to him, I asked him how he was." The reciprocality of this encounter, so easily accepted and so easily offered, was surprising because much religious rhetoric aims to prove an ideological point about Jesus of Nazareth, rather than engage with him.

Some responses to the engagement with Jesus demonstrated the environments of love within which the students obviously lived: "When Jesus said hello and knew my name, it was like my dad does when I come home from school. When he put his hand on my head, it felt like home."

An encounter that has stayed with me ever since it happened was with a boy who was soon to make his confirmation. He was a happy person, easy with himself and his classmates. When we were talking about meeting Jesus and engaging with him, he said, "When I met Jesus, he knew my name, and I was thinking about this as we walked along. When you told us that we could say anything we wanted to him, I said, 'How do I know you are who you say you are?'" This struck me as christologically pristine in its inquiry, and I asked whether Jesus had responded. The pupil said, "Yeah, he looked at me and he told me the story of my life." I asked how that felt and he said, "Nice."

I have a friend, Jenny, and she has frequently played on the borders of religion. Her interest and inquiry are both deep, but she, because she never tired of the capacity to tell the truth plainly, has often not found herself welcome deeper into the borders of religion. One time, a preacher came to her and said, "God has told me to tell you something." The message was given, and Jenny felt moved that God would have cared enough about her to say something to her. She treasured this moment. A few months later, she was telling this story to a friend, and her friend said, "Oh, the preacher said the same thing to me and told me the same thing." Jenny found out that this was a regular line of the preacher's. Her disappointment was enormous. When she told me this, Jenny said that of all the desires she's had in her life, the desire to hear something from the God that she sometimes believes in is among the deepest desires she knows.

So what then is to be done with an experience like that small boy's? Jenny was in my mind as I heard him say that he had experienced, in his imagination, Jesus looking at him and telling him the story of his life. I thought that there are people who ache for such experiences. Yet I was aware that to burden this pupil with my reading of his experience would be unfair and irresponsible. I said, "That's a lovely experience. You might want to think about it every once in a while as you come to your confirmation." He said, "OK," and then said, "Can I color?" I said, "Of course you can."

I met this same boy a few months later and asked him if he'd remembered what he'd said at our previous time together, and he said, "Oh yeah, something about Jesus and my story, wasn't it?"

♀

In his book *Inventing Ireland,* Declan Kiberd makes the point that a root meaning of *translate* was "conquer." It strikes me that in translating the young boy's experience of his imagination into something of wide value, I was playing with the dangerous art of conquering or colonization. To translate his experience to something wide is to run the risk of telling him what it meant, and in truth, he is the only one who can say what it meant, if anything.

I asked a group once, "What was Jesus like as a person? How would you describe him?" and the answers have stayed with me. "He had a big personality," said one. "He is reassuring and happy," said another, and yet another, "He looked a wee bit scruffy." Another said, "He got in a bus at the end of our talk and went away," and another said, "Respectable."

I asked this child what she meant by "respectable" and had the pleasure of being witness to a long moment of silence as she thought about what she meant. She said, "I don't mean he was stuffy. I mean that he was good at respecting people." Another pupil said the same thing in a different way: "He listened and he didn't butt in." Another one said, "He's like a therapist." I asked "What's that?" and he said, "I don't know, but I think they listen."

In my year of working at the De La Salle Pastoral Centre, there were three times that participants said that Jesus demonstrated respect. They each articulated it in different ways, but it always caught my attention. I was careful not to use the word in any introductions—I'm suspicious of the word *respect* in its imperative form—and so was always curious to know what it meant when it was used. The answers were intriguing—that they felt they could say what they wanted and would be listened to. They said that Jesus wasn't trying to argue with them or tell them to grow up.

One young person said that Jesus was Black and wore a suit, and another said he was a comfortable kind of man, trustable, who'd keep your secrets. One young girl said, "Being with Jesus was like, it was like, it was like sitting next to a cozy fire." I thought of all the words being used that day around the world to describe Jesus of Nazareth and wondered if any would surpass those. She reminded me of Oscar Wilde who, while he was imprisoned, wrote in the letter now known as *De Profundis*:

> At Christmas I managed to get hold of a Greek Testament, and every morning, after I had cleaned my cell and polished my tins, I read a little of the Gospels, a dozen verses taken by chance anywhere. It is a delightful way of opening the day. Every one, even in a turbulent, ill-disciplined life, should do the same. Endless repetition, in and out of season, has spoiled for us the freshness, the naïveté, the simple romantic charm of the Gospels. We hear them read far too often and far too badly, and all repetition is anti-spiritual. When one returns to the Greek; it is like going into a garden of lilies out of some narrow and dark house.

A friend asked me once whether I had any disquiet in speaking with children about religion, knowing that so much damage is done to integrity in the name of religion. I admitted that I did and that

I probably overstated how much of the imagination was in these exercises to the pupils and understated the soul. Like many good things, the positive potential of such experiences of the imagination is matched only by its detrimental potential if led poorly. Never have I taken a job more seriously than in hearing the stories of young people's inner walks with the Jesus of their imagination.

My own cautions were often foiled, however. Once, a pupil—in fact, the same one who had described Jesus as a cozy fireplace—said, "Pádraig, you know how you tell us this is just our imagination? Well, I'm wondering if it's a wee bit more than that."

I always tried to mention that this experience was a journey of the imagination and tie it in with the truth that the imagination is always there, so if they decided in a week, a year, a decade, or a lifetime from now to return to the place of walking, they would always be as welcome as they were in that moment. "He was happy to see me," one pupil had said when I asked her what Jesus was like, and it was a beautiful thought that the imagination might, for a moment, be perceiving something true.

Hello to the little moment of truth.

◉

Here is, as near as I could remember it, a transcript of something a twelve-year-old girl said one day:

> In our parish we are having a parish mission. So the
> priest has invited some youth workers to come and

talk at all the masses about religion and God and Jesus and all. Last Sunday a woman got up to say something during the homily and she said that she was going to tell a story about God that the children would love.

She told us this story about the station master of a train station. The station master saw that a train was coming along and saw that the line was broken. If he didn't change the line that the train was on, then the train would go off a cliff and everyone would die. So he needed to change the line, but he saw that his son was playing on the other line, the safe one. So he had to decide if he'd save the people or save his son. He saved the people.

The woman ended the story and said: "That's what God's love is like. He saved us instead of his son." She said, "That's a story that I know the young people will love."

I thought it was a stupid story because it just made me worry that my daddy is going to murder me.

The clarity of this girl's analysis of the story was compelling. She had understood the flaw at the heart of the anecdote and was applying a critique appropriate to both the words of the woman who spoke as well as the words often spoken in Christianity about the purpose of Jesus's death. Many theologians—many times this girl's age—would agree with her. It was clear that she was, as we'd say in Cork, not backward about being forward—she said what she thought when she thought it. I thought she was marvelous. I asked her if she sometimes got into trouble in school for saying what she thought. She looked at me, as if amazed that I might have perceived this about her character, and said, "All. The. Time." I said, "Well, take it from me, you've got good things to say. Keep saying them," and she looked puzzled but pleased.

Hello to being right. It's not always easy.

♀

In 2013, during a residency with the Uniting Church of Australia, based in Melbourne, I worked—and lodged—with the storyteller Julie Perrin, and together we ran some Ignatian prayer sessions in a local church. There was a small cohort of young people who attended every week for four weeks, and over the time we built up friendship and exchange. Each week we sounded a prayer bell and sat around a small focus—a focus that grew as the weeks went by because the participants responded warmly to the invitation to bring what they wanted to put into the center. We ended up with photographs, a dried insect, and music memorabilia among the icons and prayer bowls and candles. One teenage boy said that in his first imagination walk, he was walking through the woods but that it was worrying because the pathway kept changing. He found himself, eventually, in a dell, where he met Jesus. He said that Jesus asked him three questions:

Hello to the imagination

How would you describe today?

Have you seen anything interesting along the way?

And:

Is it working?

These questions, so grounded in the moment, felt like an invitation to mindfulness. I thought of and praised the imagination that is so full of insight. Knowing that the pathways change all the time, for teenagers and others too, he had found questions that invited stories of the moment and an evaluation of those stories based on whether they are working. Working for what? I don't know; he'd need to answer for himself.

◉

While working as a chaplain, I always introduced myself to pupils as Pádraig—that was the practice in the center that Margaret runs with such love. However, pupils so used to calling adults "Sir" or "Miss" often just returned to default. One time one of them said, "Sir, do you like me?"

I answered happily, "I think you're great." The boy who'd asked then turned to his friend and said, with small triumph, "See? I told you." They moved on and I was left pleasantly bewildered about the context of the question. It may have been that one boy said to the other that nobody liked him, so he asked the nearest person whether they liked him in order to prove his classmate wrong. Or it may have been that they said, "That eejit likes everybody. Ask him and see." I have no idea, and I like that unfinished circle of that story and the truth that a question asked is a question honored. How many of us, I wonder, have never had the bravery to ask such a question so boldly and bravely? While in the moment it didn't seem to cost the boy much—he seemed like a happy child—I've always wondered what untold stories accompanied the exchange.

Hello to the bravery to ask an honest question.

♀

Another time, a young girl—as enjoyably outspoken as her atonement-critiquing counterpart—interrupted me while I was speaking. I must have been boring her, and she had a question that she wanted me to answer. "Pádraig," she said with authority. "Answer me a question: God made us all, right?" I wasn't entirely sure where her rhetoric was going to take me, but I decided to go along for the ride. "Yes," I said. "And God loves us, right?" Again, I was unsure, but I said, "Yes." "Answer me this," she continued. "Why did God make Protestants?"

Oh, the stories beneath questions.

I wanted to know more, so asked her to tell me a bit more about where the story was coming from. She said, and this is a quote, "Well, they hate us and they hate him." I happened to know that she loved football and was highly skilled at it. I said, "I know a lot of Protestants who'd love to have you on their team." "Really?" she asked, and she seemed surprised. Then she rallied and said, "And what about French people? What God made them?"

Here, in the mind of her, was a litany of truths learned well. She had learned—how could she not, given the history of Belfast—that if you believe someone hates you, then they must also hate your God, and possibly are even made by another God. This extended not only to hate but also to difference. She told me that she'd recently gone on a trip to France and had seen a lot of French people walking around speaking French, and she wondered, "What God made them?" She had learned the lessons of Ireland well, and she asked questions with all the limitations and imagination of truth. If God is for you, who can be against you? wrote the writer of the letter to the Romans. This girl had been taught a lesson by her community, and she had learned it well. If God is for you, then who is he against?

Hello to the gods of our creation.

♀

I've done these journeys of prayer with groups of adults too. One time, I was with a group of people on a retreat. The retreat was somewhat unusual because it was mostly made up of people from Pentecostal denominations on a contemplative retreat run by a Catholic. They didn't know—and I wasn't in the position of safety to tell them—that they were on a retreat run by a gay Catholic, and what didn't harm them didn't hurt them, so we had a wonderful time of prayer and connection.

We explored a particular text from the Gospel of Luke— where a woman makes her own way into the house of a Pharisee, a house where Jesus is eating. The woman cries and shows extravagance to Jesus, and the Pharisee judges Jesus for his association with the woman.

One of the participants on the retreat—a farmer from rural New Zealand, a woman whose religion needed to be as sharp as the seasons—said that she'd been spending time with the story. She was trying to picture the whole scene, and she'd tried to envision it as if she were a servant standing in the corner, watching the event take place. But without any possibility of control, she found herself immersed in the person of the Pharisee. She was the Pharisee, watching the whole thing take place—she saw Jesus and she saw the woman who was weeping at the feet of Jesus, pouring extravagant oil on his feet and wiping the oil and tears with her hair and hands. The farmer said that she was overcome with jealousy. "Why can't I ever be like that? Why can't I ever let it all spill out and say how I feel?" she found herself asking.

She had used her imagination in this way because I'd suggested that the participants on the retreat find a Gospel story and enter into it. I'd suggested a few questions, and as she finished the story, she apologized because she didn't think she'd asked enough of the questions that I'd suggested. She, however, had landed on a much more important truth than my limited questions could embody. Somewhere, I remember being told—although I've never been able to verify it—that Ignatius of Loyola instructed his followers on such matters by saying that if something unexpected happens in your prayer, then you should pay attention to it. Well, I say that I heard that Ignatius said it. Maybe I made that up so that it'd stay with me. Either way, the farmer's experience of her own desire was overwhelming.

Hello to what we do not expect.

Hello to the imagination.

○

A question posed by Ignatius is seemingly simple but, at the heart of it, is among the most difficult of questions to answer. "What do you want?" is the question. What do we want with our lives? What do we want with our work? What do we want with our failures, with our reputations, with our friendships and achievements? What do we want in our faith and in the truth of our body?

What do you want?

It is a question that requires simple engagement with the truth—brave, guileless, honest truth.

Working as a chaplain with young people was a regular reminder of how compelling guilelessness is. Guile, my *Dictionary of Etymology* tells me, meaning crafty deceit, is probably borrowed from the Frankish word meaning "trick" or from the Old Frisian, meaning "sorcery." This was talk about God with no tricks, and the truths told were grander than the small bodies that told them.

○

One of the exercises I did with teenage students was one where, on the walk with Jesus, the student and Jesus passed by four people. They passed by a person who was injured, a person who was excluded, a person who was ill, and a person who was lonely. It tied in with the theme of the day, which was "Who is my neighbor?" While many of the responses were to be expected (healed the sick, etc.), they were often as surprising as they were predictable. In one student's mind, it all became clear. He said that he and Jesus were walking, and when Jesus saw the bullied person, he sat next to them, and he cured the injured person, and he got the sick person something to drink. However, when they came to the lonely person, he mentioned the name of a girl and added, by way of an explanatory gloss, "She's a wee girl I have a fancy for, sir." Then he told me that he'd said to Jesus, "Stay you here. I'll take over now."

This, to me, was an experience where the Jesus of his imagination would have been the recipient of the surprise. But it speaks it so well. Once, years ago, I got a card from the parents of a young man I had been doing some work with. The card said, "Our faith tells us to be thankful at all times, so we are sending you this card to say thanks." I wondered who made those abysmal cards, and I also wondered if I could find a card that said, "Don't bother." The young man at the De La Salle Pastoral Centre had understood something that the card writers didn't. Our faith is to guide us so that we can move from merely doing what is good because we trust the source to doing what is good—maybe because we know it's good, or maybe because we like it, or maybe because we just do it. We can move beyond "I'm doing this because God tells me" to "I'm doing this because it's good." Some people don't need the first step. Others get stuck there. The call is to go beyond it, with all the courage and critique that that entails. "I pray God rid me of God," Peter Rollins is fond of quoting. Our ideas of God sometimes get in the way of the truth that we are already acting upon, and God is the excuse that hides the lie. The deepest impulse of religion is to move from obligation to something entirely more intuitive—the telling of truth, the doing of truth, the living of a life, the confrontation of what we truly want.

Hello to God, who leaves us to do what we want.

I always liked asking young people how they ended their walk with Jesus. "How did you say goodbye to Jesus?" I asked one young person. "I hugged him and he called a taxi," she answered. And another had heard the Jesus of his imagination say, "I'll probably see you again."

Hello to saying goodbye.

Is It Working?

When you've been alive for only
five thousand
eight hundred
and twenty-nine days

The pathways are
rarely clear
here where
the roads keep changing.

What makes sense
on one day
makes none
the next.

And so
to avoid exhaustion
and to deepen rest
ask yourself

these questions.
How would you
describe today?
And

Have you seen
anything interesting
on the way?
And

Is it working?
Is it working?
Always
Is it working?

4

Hello to trouble

Years ago, I had a dream. In the dream, I was on a hillside, dreamwalking in a daze because I'd been condemned to death. On the hillside I met a ghost and asked one question—"How am I going to die?"—and the ghost told me that I would walk into a cave, a large cave, and I would sit. In the cave was a chasm, and once I had sat down, the chasm would fill with flames and I would choke from the smoke of the flames.

In the dream, I went to the cave. My body still remembers the rattling of fear at that entrance. At the entrance, I looked back and I noticed that my best friend was walking away, weeping because I couldn't be helped.

I woke up.

It was just the latest in a lifetime of nightmares about caves and caverns and tombs. My own name—Ó Tuama—means "tomb." If you read the Gospels in Irish it is to the empty *tuama* that Mary Magdalene goes. Ó Tuama, or its English derivatives Twomey, Twoomey, Toomey, is a popular name in Cork. I've heard—although I'm not sure if this is correct—that the name comes from North Cork, where there are some caves in a hillside.

In the Shelter

Jung wrote, "In the cave, I discovered remains of a primitive culture, that is, the world of the primitive man within myself—a world which can scarcely be reached or illuminated by consciousness." At the time of the deathcave dream, I was going to a psychotherapist on a weekly basis. The dream—I think a lifetime might only bring a handful of such dreams—happened in the hours between a Saturday night and a Sunday morning. I told the psychotherapist about the dream the next week. I had written it down and described as much as I could. After I had finished, he was quiet for a while and asked, "What was in the cave?"

This was all in Australia, the other side of the world. I had gone there because it was the furthest place I could think of to go. As I spoke about the dream, I knew that there was no reason why, awake, I would fear to look around the inside of that cave. But the logic of wakefulness is often undone by the animal unconscious. It seems that I was willing to travel a long way to avoid the entrance to the cave, even to the end of the world.

Early in my time with the psychotherapist, I was waiting in the reception area with other clients for other appointments. I was trying to avoid eye contact, so I busied myself with the brochure stand. Once I found a brochure with some words in Irish. "*Ar scáth a chéile a mhaireas na daoine,*" the brochure said. It was an advertisement for an upcoming conference, and the conference organizers used an Irish saying that translates in one way as "It is in the shelter of each other that the people live." Another way to translate it is "It is in the shadow of each other that the people live." The word *scáth* can mean both shelter and shadow.

Hello to trouble

I was surprised to find the language of my childhood ten thousand miles from where I'd grown up. Before I'd started school I had spent two years at a playgroup run by a woman who spoke little English, so by the time I started formal schooling I was in the happy dilemma of not knowing what languages were, even though I spoke two. When I started school, the teacher introduced the idea of us learning the Irish language. She said some words. I felt like I was getting it wrong because she had told us we were to learn new words, but I already understood the new words. It is one thing not to understand. It is another thing not to understand that you've already understood. I've loved the Irish language since I was a child, and here, in a waiting room half a world away, a quarter of a century later, I found a tongue I understood.

I told the psychotherapist about the saying and about how *scáth* was both "shelter" and "shadow." He asked me if the cave, the *tuama*, the place of death, could be both a shelter and a shadow, a place for the living as well as a place for the condemned. He—even if only in language—had a point. And language is sometimes enough for a start.

I stepped inside the cave and looked around.

Hello to the shadow and the shelter.

Hello to the *scáth*.

📍

Ar scáth a chéile a mhaireas na daoine.

It is in the shelter of each other that the people live. It is also in the shadow of each other that the people live. It could also mean

93

"Our shelter can be our shadow" or even "What shelters me may shadow you." The poet Micheal O'Siadhail, also a linguist, wrote to me once that *scáth* is related to a Norwegian word for "mist." He wrote, "I wonder if the wisdom in this proverb demands a kind of discernment, a peering through the blur of ordinary living to decide when closeness overshadows and when it protects."

We can do beautiful things and terrible things to ourselves and to those we consider to be "our others." We know this everywhere; in Belfast, neighbors have known—and sometimes caused—their neighbors' terror and also their trouble, their sheltering and their shadowing, their radiances and their rages.

The word "shadow" in Old English is *sceadu*, meaning "darkness" or "protection," and the Old English for "shelter" might also have meant "shield." One of the ancient Hebrew words for shelter is *sel*—it also means "shadow" as well as "transitoriness." A Greek word for shadow, *skia*, implies "foreshadowing," and its sister word *skenoo* can mean "shelter" or "tent dwelling."

The Gospel of John uses these words at the beginning. The word became flesh and tent dwelled among us. The word became flesh and made his shadow and his shelter here.

Words have meaning. Words have power. Words shape the tents we live in and the places we depart from. They contain and they constrain. But anyway, in the midst of all this multilingual sheltering and shadowing, god-talk and babbling, I am remembering what Declan Kiberd meant when he wrote that all translations are little colonizations. It's baffling that we manage to understand each other at all.

Hello to trouble

I moved to Belfast in 2003. At that point, I had had a nomadic decade, having moved from Cork to Dublin and then Switzerland and Australia, with short and long jaunts in Lithuania, Uganda, and the Philippines along the way. By the time I moved to Belfast, I was tired of moving and determined to settle: a good thing, too—I had never experienced as much culture shock in my life. Some people spoke to me as a fellow Irishman; others insisted I was a foreigner.

Hello to the shock of surprise.

Hello to the echo of trouble.

◉

For my first few years in Belfast, I found myself in a certain amount of shock. I knew how to read the etymology of the place names—I was only a hundred miles up the road from Dublin and a drive away from Cork. I was on the same island of Ireland that I'd grown up in, but depending on whom I was speaking to, I was either a local or a foreigner.

"I love Cork," one man said to me. "It's a great county."

"Oh, you're from Ireland?" another man said to me. "I was in Finland once."

People who grew up here say that they learned early the skill of discerning whether someone was from their side or the other side. It's all in the small slips of the tongue, I hear. If you say "Northern Ireland" or "the North," if you refer to the island of Britain as "the mainland" or "across the water," whether you aspirate the letter "h" or not when you spell "hell," if you offer "a prayer" or "to pray," what school uniform you wear, what school you refer to, whether you go to mass or church, whether you carry a Bible to the house of worship, and what things you hush at.

I once wrote a poem called "[the] north[ern] [of] ireland." It was a poem designed to annoy everybody.

What do you have when you don't have a shared name for a place? You have possibility.

The peace accord signed on Good Friday in 1998 is a fascinating piece of constitutional artistry. It enshrines, in perpetuity, the right for citizens of the jurisdiction in the northeastern corner of Ireland to hold multiple identities. People born into this space can be British citizens or Irish citizens or both. Everybody born here has the right to two passports. I've heard people refer to the north of Ireland as the unwanted offspring between two neighboring nations.

While I knew, before moving to Belfast, that this was the dynamic I'd experience, nothing had prepared me for my own feelings about it. On my first night in Belfast, I looked out of my back window and there was a small boy, wrapped in an Irish flag, standing on the back wall of my garden. He was looking out toward a Protestant area and singing, "Burn, burn, burn ye bastards" to the tune of "What Shall We Do with a Drunken Sailor?" This was neither a childhood nor a flag that I recognized.

Hello to what you do not recognize.

So I was in need of survival. For a few years, I held an occasional meal in my house for others who'd moved up from the Republic of Ireland, the Freestate, the South—there are so many names to refer to our two jurisdictions—to the North. At each meal, we'd pose a question and would reflect on it. One time, we asked, "How does living in the North change your relationship to the Irish flag?" and another time we asked, "How do you feel about people in the South who have strong feelings about the North but who've never lived here?" and another time we asked, "Do you feel like a foreigner here? Do you feel like a local? Do you feel something else?" Even the terminology of the questions was clumsy. I wasn't posing the questions as an exercise in pristine political syntax. I was posing them because I needed to think about them in order to survive. I'd grown up loving the Irish language, Irish poetry, Irish music and dance, and now I was living in a place, on the same island, where those things existed in some quarters as a local expression of culture but were understood, in other quarters, as a foreign thing, perhaps even a suspicious thing.

The nights of mealtimes were a survival. Of course, the food was also good—usually everybody had to bring food that was either green, white, or orange, the colors of the Irish flag—and the company was great. We had Catholics from the South, Protestants from the South, as well as Catholics who'd become Protestants or Protestants who'd become Catholics.

How do you negotiate the recalibration of your national identity? With friends, discussion, good food, politics, argument, and commitment. I know of no other way. I knew of brave Protestants who'd lived their lives in the shadow of grief—people whose familial lives had been ripped by murder—they looked to Britain for identity, they felt more at home in Scotland than they did in Dublin, and their friendship was more important to me than a shared national identity, even in this peculiar shared space.

In the Shelter

The notion of reciprocality is an important one. For the shared space of Northern Ireland, our belonging is found by a reciprocal relationship of national, cultural, and social identities based on relationship, acknowledgment of pain, and commitment for a different present leading to a different future. It's as if the right answer to the question "What country are you from?" is "Well, let me tell you a story." In a strange way, it is among the brightest kinds of political ideology that might offer hope to other regions of contested space, and there are many. There are borderlands in every continent that are disputed, with languages, families, and cultures being split by political lines drawn on a map. The lines have changed from time to time, and so has the pain—it's gotten deeper. The project of this part of the North of Ireland points to the fact that no matter what government has territorial claim over it, the right will remain—people here have the right to choose between two national identities, or they can choose both.

It is as if a new color has been proposed for a map of the world, the map of previously contested space that can now be considered shared space. This color could be appropriate to frontiers all around the world. But this model is new, and we are at the feet of something bright, but it's so big we haven't found the way to acknowledge it yet.

It is an exercise in the art of compromise, and compromise, for many, is like death. But death happens anyway. So what do we do?

Hello to the resented art of compromise.

Hello to trouble

○

I do not propose welcoming the darkness of bereavement, especially in light of deaths that are marked as a political victory. While I appreciate the character of death in Philip Pullman's epic His Dark Materials trilogy, or in Zuzak's *The Book Thief*, and while I love John O'Donohue's stories about death in *Anam Cara*, I have never faced my own death or the murder of someone I love. I don't know whether words of welcome toward death are based on love or fear, expediency or exorcism. But the often unwelcome fact is that death is there, and death sometimes walks a slow predictable path, and other times is there and gone before you'd had time to think about it. This is not a fact that I like, but it is a fact.

Hello to the facts of life.

Hello to the facts of death.

○

The Gospel character of Judas is worthy of attention. As with all characters, there are different entry points to the story about him. If one particular reading of him is taken, he is the antipurpose to the purpose of God in Jesus of Nazareth. If another reading is taken, he is a thief who was in with the crowd of disciples for his own selfish purposes.

Both of these readings are convenient because they paint a clear picture. He is like Voldemort or Sauron or any number of the malevolent characters in the texts by which we feed our lives and imagination. It is clear, however, that this convenience needs to be inconvenienced. It is usually fruitful to assume that most people do what seems reasonable to them at the time, most of the time.

I am feeling the need to repeat myself, probably for my own benefit.

Most people do what seems reasonable to them at the time, most of the time.

Taking this into account, what was reasonable about betraying Jesus of Nazareth? Matthew, Mark, Luke, and John each introduce Judas as the disciple who was to betray Jesus. The writer of John's Gospel portrays Judas as a thief, a man who used to help himself to the funds in the common purse. With such an introduction, his name may as well be written in blood, and the mindset of the reader of the Gospels is firm. The good are yet to be discerned, but the bad is clear: the bad is Judas.

The word in Greek for "betray" is *paradidōmi*. It's a curious word, because depending on the context, usage, or place in the sentence it can mean "handed over" or "entrusted" or even "ripe."

I reflect on this because I think the story of Judas has something to teach us, which is that the introduction to the shadowed part of our own lives, our own communities, our own societies and religions has much to teach us. To deny that there is an underbelly to good motivations or to our seemingly innocent actions is to be in denial about the complexity of human interactions. It seems ludicrous to imagine that Judas, having spent a significant period of time around Jesus, simply decided to throw it all away for the benefit of silver.

Hello to trouble

Harry Clarke is one of Ireland's most honored artists and is particularly praised for his stained glass artwork. In the Crawford Art Gallery in Cork, the panel *St. Brendan and the Unhappy Judas* is permanently exhibited. In it, St. Brendan, hair streaming back from a fresh sea breeze, braves the waves on a boat with some similarly solemn-faced companions. Outside of the boat is a naked—and presumably unhappy—Judas. Judas is frozen by waves and scalded by flames. As a teenager, I spent a lot of time in the gallery and this picture always undid me. Here was someone wrapped in the eternal flame of punishment.

How do we understand the character of Judas without resorting to the most simplistic form of human understanding? Most people do what seems reasonable to them at the time, most of the time. Was this the time when somebody did what seemed unreasonable to them, even at the time?

Matthew's Gospel seems to sketch the most multidimensional Judas of the lot. In it, Judas had approached the authorities and asked what they'd give him if he gave Jesus into their hands. They gave him money, and Judas began looking for an opportunity to betray him. There's that word again: *betrayal, hand over, entrust, ripe*. There's a thought—popular among plenty of scholars—that Judas wished for a revolution and thought that what the people needed was a hero, and what a hero needs is a threat, and what a threat needs is a public arrest. While it's speculation, it's worthwhile speculation, because perhaps Judas was like us, believing that public attention is good attention and that therefore public attention on Jesus would focus the people on undoing the arrest and threatening the power of the powerful. Who knows? It's all speculation, but it can go a long way to explaining what happened next.

In Matthew's Gospel, when Judas sees that Jesus has been condemned, he returns the silver to the people who'd given it to him. Not only that, but he repents. Given that the Gospel texts are relatively short, every word has to be weighed heavily, so that the writer of Matthew notes that "when Judas, his betrayer, saw that Jesus was condemned, he repented and brought back the thirty pieces." What a repentance. But we do not remember Judas the repenter, we remember Judas the betrayer. We do not weigh his actions as he weighed his actions. The thing that caused his repentance was that Jesus had been condemned. This seems to indicate that his actions, misguided as they were and devastating as their consequences were, were intended for something other than condemnation. A riot? A revolution, perhaps? Or something else entirely.

Hello to the failure of our national intentions.

In any event, even those whose silver Judas had taken were reluctant to use the returned thirty pieces for holy purposes. So they used it to buy a field to bury foreigners. Judas hanged himself, and all this is inserted by Matthew before Jesus has even met Pilate. Judas saw the lay of the land, it seemed. Luke tells the story of Judas's death differently in the second of his works—the Acts of the Apostles—where he tells that Judas bought a field from the spoils of betrayal but that he tripped in that field and burst open in the middle and his bowels rushed out, and so the field was therefore known as a field of blood. The word for "bowels" here is *splagchnon*. In Greek syntax, the bodily location for compassion, tenderness, and affection is not the heart, but the bowels. For Luke, it is as if he is implying that the final vestige of anything good had to flee the body of Judas and that it did so by bursting, alien-like, from the body of him, causing his death and the corruption of a field.

What does all this have to say? It is to say that the shadows have much to teach us and that the story we tell of our shadows is sometimes the convenient story that seeks to distance the shared location between intention and impact. The awful truth is that our mixed intentions sometimes have the unmixed impact of terror. It doesn't justify the intention, but it goes a long way toward creating understanding.

Hello to the awful shadow. It has much to teach us.

♀

I was walking around Belfast once and I saw a woman pushing a child in a stroller. It was a gray day, and people were moving from one place to another, they were buying credit for their phones and matches for cigarettes, milk for tea, and they were paying bills.

The woman was pushing the stroller, and in it there was a two-year-old child, and the child was squirming and making complaining noises. The woman stopped, walked around so she could see the face of the child, and screamed, "I fucking hate you."

She screamed her hate loudly.

Life in the city continued. People continued to buy food and items to make their homes look good. People wondered if they could afford a bill and people admired clothes in shop windows.

In the Shelter

This is not a story particular to Belfast. It could happen on any street in any city. It is not a story particular to one economic class either. This was ten years ago. I am sure that child is still alive.

Hello to hatred.

The truth we hear from the story of the woman with the child is that we all have our breaking points, and when we break we say more about ourselves than about the one who is the victim of our breaking. I will fall, and in my falling, I will drag you with me, and I will drag you to my own hell with me. It is an awful truth, but it is a truth lived out in most—although I want to say every—human experience. Can we stop it? I don't know, I don't think so, but I think we can find a way to name it, to greet it, and acknowledge it.

Hello to what we hate. It has much to tell us.

What is the saddest thing about this story? Is it the hate, or the words chosen? Is it that she chose the word *fucking*? I know that her sentiment is not unusual—either in the streets of Belfast or in the suburbs of any city. To raise a child, I am told, is a long exercise in facing your own failure. She may have gone home and held that child long enough to forgive herself and hope that the child's mind was elastic enough to add love to failure. Who knows? Either way, she's not alone, and if you have never felt like that toward another human, you are not far from someone who has.

The woman with the child was experiencing a kind of death, the kind of death that turns colors to gray and turns love to resentment; the kind of death that feels like asthma, a slow constricting of the pathways to air. She was falling and the only way to know how to make sense of her falling was to scream loudly, in a public space. It was a small concerto of chaos, and there was a stage and there was an audience of one and a streetful of an audience to the audience of one. *Audience* comes from a word for "listening," and the listening can sometimes speak and the audiences were being asked for something more—these audiences were being asked to contribute to the script.

I don't know what the contribution could have been, but I hope that somebody who knew her might have found the words to join her in her fall. Not every fall needs to be final; for some it can be a fall into truth or, better still, rest.

So much of our activities—even our spiritual activities—are about exorcising our own screaming shadows from ourselves. Leonard Cohen, in one of his poems from *Book of Mercy*, writes in praise of the integrity of falling: "And in his fall he hears his heart cry out, his heart explains why he is falling, why he had to fall, and he gives over to the fall. Blessed are you, clasp of the falling."

Whenever I think of the woman, I hope that in her own fury she could hear something of her need. I think of her child, a teenager now, and I hope that they have found themselves clasped by something bigger than their fall.

> Blessed are you, embrace of the falling, foundation
> of the light, master of the human accident.

In the years leading up to moving to Belfast, I discovered a love for groupwork—bringing people together to discuss their differences, disagreements, griefs, and furies. It functioned, accidentally, as a preparation for moving to Belfast, where those skills—and all the associated limitations—were pushed and honed and highlighted. Groups are, to state the obvious, made of people; groups work because of brave and powerful people who make groupwork work.

I grew in my love of groups through the Corrymeela Community, a Christian community of peace that began in 1965 as the Troubles were brewing. They were demonstrating their commitment to using the arts in public dialogue and asked if I would be poet in residence for some new groups that were beginning. I was used to helping people discuss theological or cultural differences, but here I was helping groups tell stories of grief and stories of trouble, stories of accusation and stories of hope.

Hello to inadequacy.

I was a gay man working mostly in the field of religion, and on reflection, the experience of secrecy and hidden mines of dignity taught me something. On some levels, I was prepared for what I encountered, and on other levels, nothing could have prepared me for what was to come. I was an Irishman who was in a story of Ireland that was new to my bones.

In these groups, we have shelter and we have shadow; we have shade and darkness. We have colonization, translation, languages, shields, and transitoriness. We have visors to shade and we have places to escape from. We have trust and foreshadowing. We have neighbors knowing each other's troubles and we have neighbors who do not speak to neighbors because they share neither land nor story, languages nor shelter. Here we have borders and also the limitations of language. We meet each other, and we fumble for words—words that contain and constrain—words we use to tell each other some truths. Welcome to Belfast.

I worked with Jonny McEwen, an artist, on a course that he had codesigned. The course brought people from neighboring, but not-neighborly, suburbs to think about their geography. We typically had a group of fifteen people meeting weekly for seven to ten weeks initially. The project worked best when a group of Catholic people met for a course of their own while, concurrently, a group of Protestant people were also meeting. Following these single-identity group experiences, everybody was invited to join a joint program that would run, again, for seven to ten weeks.

People penciled street maps on beautiful, high-quality paper; they colored in the places where they regularly go, and blanked out places they would not, or could not, go. They wrote the stories of their neighborhoods on the maps they drew, and then made history markings on their own cartography. They thought about the stories that paved the streets of their own maps, and they told the stories to each other first and then, eventually, to other groups—once they had met for long enough to feel safe.

On one occasion, someone scribbled on a street corner of a map. She scribbled so hard that the pencil became blunt and the paper wore thin. There was such strength in the scribble.

Hello to the scribble of chaos.

(As I was writing "hello" here, I made a mistake and wrote "helo" and the autocorrect on my computer changed it to "help," and when I tried to correct it, it changed it to "hell." And then I thought how correct Arundhati Roy was when she wrote that sometimes we write stories and sometimes stories write us.)

9

The rooms where we gathered were always warm, and we never sat in an open circle. We always sat around tables that were populated with safety—tea, coffee, milk, sugar, pots, biscuits, and half-eaten sandwiches. Why this populated space? Because it's ordinary, because it echoes the tables we sit at in our own homes, because too much empty space has been our problem, not our solution. There have been too many lives lost and too many stories blanked.

The Irish word *Trioblóid* is rendered as "Troubles" in English, but it really means "Bereavements." During the years of the Troubles, there were too many deaths that were deemed "so political" that their stories still cannot be told out loud. We have lived with the silence of grief and the deadening silence of silenced grief. We have lived with the silence of governments, politicians, clergy, community leaders, and community members. People have been killed, and sometimes bodies have been hidden and, in my mind, there is too much damned empty space. Now is not the time for emptiness in the center of these communities. Now is the time for discovering, recovering, talking, and telling, around tables with cups of tea, food, humanity, and a bit of shared normality in the wake of abnormal abominations.

When the Irish journalist Olivia O'Leary addressed the audience in London during the first state visit of an Irish president to Britain, she noted the long and mixed history of the Irish and British people. She mentioned travels and language and shared cultural heritages. She noted how many—if not most—homes in Ireland receive the broadcasts of the BBC, and she further noted, with glee, that Irish people have received these broadcasts without paying the BBC license fee. She got a delicious round of applause for this insight, a round of applause that continued when she considered this eavesdropping pastime as a "down payment on the debts of empire." It was evidence of her charm and insight and made a serious point amid the amusement.

How much does empire cost?
Land and language and blood and history and futures and present.
How much does resistance cost?
Land and language and blood and history and futures and present.
How to weigh them both?
Land and language and blood and history and futures and present.

Hello to the complicated art of living with one another.

♀

So we tell stories of streets. We remember people long dead and we say their names out loud. We remember streets destroyed and streets rebuilt and renamed. We remember the shelter found in a corner sweetshop whose owner valued safety. We remember the doctor's office that seemed miles from the chaos on the street below. We remember the shelter of the woman whose door was always open and whose kettle was always on, and the long shadow of the threat given to a taxi driver's family. We gather together in little rooms and speak stories and truth. We voice accusation, grief, and glory; we remember shelter; and we make room for scribbles whose shadow we may not emerge from.

There are questions about how to get the right people into the programs of storytelling in places like Belfast that are trying to recover from conflict. But the right people are not on a list. It's less about having the right people and more about finding ways of listening, about helping roomfuls of people to hear the chord, or the "dischord," being played by the tension of stories in the room. Sometimes, in a room, you can see it happen. Somebody begins to dare to believe that their story might be believed. In a place like Northern Ireland, everybody is aware that there are many who will disbelieve, deny, or devalue a story. So in rooms of groups telling stories, brave people risk telling the story that most needs to be believed to the ones who, it is to be expected, may find it the most difficult to believe.

There are many reasons to find a story difficult to believe. That shouldn't stop us from trying. For some, it is life and death. Once a person left the room. She ran for the bathroom, and I wondered if she'd come back. When she did, I wondered how best to shelter her in the room where she wouldn't welcome the exposure of a question. One of the other participants said, "I cry in the bathroom too." They shared an exchange of relief, belief, and truth that was moving to witness. All this peace work can hope for is found in that brief moment. In those generous words, we see people noticing people. We see people moving from their story to validate the experience of another story. We see how someone can use their own small tools of surviving a difficult day and help create a sense of shelter for someone whose day is crumbling. The tone with which these gestures happen is a humble tone—nobody thinks that one small kindness is going to change a life. But it might change a moment, and in that moment something small can grow. Funding programs, mediative skills, opportunities for cultural, political, and religious interchange— they all only hope for such moments when a group inclines itself kindly toward itself.

Hello to the possibilities we embody with each other.

What does *believe* mean? There's a lie in the middle of it: that's the first thing. Believe. My *Dictionary of Etymology* notes that a particular Germanic root word contributing to "believe" means "to make palatable to oneself." To be believed and to feel believed: these are deeper forms of the same thing. Curiously, the entry for "belittle" is what follows the entry for "believe" in my etymological dictionary. When the story of your country is not believed, then things are exhausting. When the differences of opinion are belittled, the story can invoke fury. We share so little in the northeastern corner of Ireland—some see the Troubles as beginning in 1967; others go back to the 1600s. Some see us as an outcrop of Britain; others see us as colonized and occupied land. Some call it Northern Ireland and others call it the North of Ireland. These aren't word games either. Depending on what you believe, death was called murder or legitimate aggression.

●

Sometimes, in the telling of stories, we injure and cure at the same time. Once, people from a village in the wake of a murder gathered and told their stories of their trauma. They got to telling other stories too, and one night we told stories of a time when we realized "I will be able to measure my life before and after this moment." People told stories of jobs, divorces, marriages, children, bodies, changes, and death. Some of the stories told were told with aching and they were heard with an echo of that ache. At the end of the night, one of the participants looked around the room. Up until that point, the group used to call itself "the two groups"—the Catholic group and the Protestant group. "Well," the woman said, looking around, "we're one group now." And she was right. Another person had left the room. For her, the timing wasn't right, and she couldn't stay. That wasn't failure; it was just a different kind of truth telling.

●

I'm told that linguists debate a particular question. One way of saying the question is "Do different languages carve out unique systems of thought, meaning, and value because of the cadences, histories, and concepts within that language?" Some say "yes." The ones who say "yes" say that because Irish has a particular word, *ochón*, to mean "croon in grief," leading to a particularity of grief expression in Irish culture. Most say that there is a deeper set of meaning indigenous to all humans, and all languages circle this deeper set of meanings. For the latter group, it doesn't matter that the Irish language has no word for "no"; we're still stubborn bastards.

Myself, I don't know how to know an answer to the linguists' question. What I do know is that I believe the woman who said "It's good to talk," and I believe the man who said "I hate it when you say that," and I believe the group who said "I'm glad the talking has begun." These groups are often battered by murder and double-battered by the disbelief of the story of the murder. They feel far from caring and feel far from therapy, health, and encounter. The ones who come to hold the story spaces come with time and techniques, but these can only go so far. It is in the shelter of the storytelling that the people live and that the people see their shadows. And sometimes the shadows are very long.

◉

Once, in a group, somebody said, "Let's have something like communion." So we did. We read words that were nearby. We read words from the prophet Ezekiel and we read words from Ted Hughes. We had the Gideon Bible and we had Ted Hughes's *Crow*. We ripped bread, talked, and instead of wine, we drank whiskey. It was cheap whiskey. It burned as it went down. We found shelter in sharp words and the shadows were made sharper by firewater.

In the Shelter

Story is a word that some people use with fairy tales. My *Dictionary of Etymology* tells me that the history of the word holds meanings of "wise man" and the verb "to see." To tell a story well is to see wisely, I say to myself. I don't know if it needs to be true, but I believe it. If a story is a beginning, there might be a place it leads to, a deeper truth telling about the essence of ourselves, and the essence of ourselves-in-relation-to-the-other, particularly the feared other. Some stories start off in rooms and end up in Narnia, Never Never Land, Wonderland, or other little hells. But if we stick with the story, it will tell us something.

We can never tell the whole story—and we never try. I don't know if the story of our griefs has an ending, only a next chapter, or, perhaps, the careful telling and retelling of the recent chapters. We tell stories in groups so that people can be believed, so that people can make meaning, so that people can carve and create kindness for another and eventually themselves.

We hope that our storytelling can be a little shelter amid the trouble.

We hope that we can tell stories of our troubles.

We hope we can say hello to our shelter.

In the Name

In the name of goodness, of love and of broken community
in the name of meaning, of feeling and I hope you don't
    screw me
in the name of darkness and light and ungraspable twilight
in the name of mealtimes and sharing and caring by firelight

In the name of action, of peace and of human redemption
in the name of eating, of drinking and table confession
in the name of sadness, regret and holy obsession
in the holy name of anger, the spirit of aggression

In the name of forgive and forget, and I hope I get over this
in the name of fathers and mothers and unholy spirits
in the name of beauty and broken and beaten up daily
in the name of seeing our creeds and believing in maybe

We gather here, a roomful of strangers
and speak of our hopeland, and talk of our danger
to make sense of our thinking, to authenticate lives
to humanize feeling and stop telling lies

In the name of philosophy, of theology and who gives a damn
in the name of employment and study and finding new family
in the name of our passions, our lovings and indecent obsessions
in the name of prayer, of worship and demon possession

In the name of solitude, of quiet and holy reflection
in the name of the lost, the lonely and the without-direction
in the name of the early and the late and the wholly ineffectual
in the name of the straight and the queer, transgender and
    bisexual

In the name of bootclogs, and boobjobs and erectile dysfunction,
in the name of schizophrenia, hysteria and obsessive compulsion
in the name of Jesus, and Mary and the mostly silent Joseph
in the name of speaking to ourselves saying "this is more than I
    can cope with"

In the name of touchup, and breakup, and of breakdown-
    and-weeping
in the name of therapy, and Prozac, and of full-hearted breathing
in the name of sadness and madness and years-since-I've-smiled
in the name of the Unknown, the Alien, and of the Wholly-in-Exile

In the name of the named and the unnamed and the names of the
    nameless
In the name of the prayers that repeat "I wish that I could change
    this"
In the name of goodness and kindness and intentionality
In the name of harbor, and shelter and family.

5

Hello to what we cannot know

On a Belfast bus a few years ago, I saw an advertisement for a religious meeting. The advertisement said,

Are you lacking Faith? Or Hope? Or Certainty?

Contact information and details of a public meeting were given, and the poster suggested that the answer to the questions posed was Jesus. It struck me that those who chose the words for the poster had, probably by mistake, told a deep truth. Usually, following the words of St. Paul in his first letter to the Corinthians, the trinity is Faith, Hope, and Love. In replacing *love* with *certainty*, much of the risk was gone. If one had to choose between love and certainty, it would be a hard choice, because we have a deep desire for both, it seems. What is it that we can truly know? And, perhaps asking the question pragmatically, what do we do with the knowledge that we have?

When I was nine years old, one of the boys in my class said that if you said the Our Father backward while looking in the mirror then your reflection would turn into the face of the devil. One of the boys—Oliver—had done it and, according to what quickly became class legend, simultaneously saw the face of Satan and vomited. I walked home that day with my friend Gavin, saying the rosary for fear of my life.

Access to the heart of all knowledge and the heart of all evil, these things haunt us, and haunt our religion.

Hello to the quest for certainty.

◉

I read Robert M. Pirsig's *Zen and the Art of Motorcycle Maintenance* with hope and expectation, because Henri Nouwen had praised it so highly. I think I was too young to appreciate it, because most of it went over my head. Or, perhaps, I wasn't yet asking the right question. The one thing I remember vividly about the book is Pirsig's discussion about how to answer the wrong question. He suggests that the Japanese word *mu* is appropriate for when the wrong question is being asked. *Mu*, he writes,

> states that the context of the question is such that a yes or no answer is in error and should not be given. "Unask the question" is what it says. *Mu* becomes appropriate when the context of the question becomes too small for the truth of the answer. When the Zen monk Joshu was asked whether a dog had a buddha nature he said "*Mu*" meaning that if he answered either way he was answering incorrectly.

Hello to what we cannot know

What is truth? Pontius Pilate asked a Galilean man about to be tortured and killed. *Mu*, said the Galilean.

Hello to the trick question.

Hello to the question behind the question.

♀

Much advertising of contemporary religious practice appeals, it seems to me, to a crude side of our desire for certainty. Knowledge, to be sure, is a good thing, but knowledge is different from certainty. If the answer to life's questions is Jesus, then it occurs to me that the wrong question might be being asked. How do I find the answer to all life's questions? Jesus. How do I end my loneliness? Jesus. How can I move from here to there? Jesus.

Hello to the wrong question.

I don't know. It may be that Jesus can help, but as a companion to courage, not as a chapter ending. If Jesus is the answer to the question I don't know I'm asking, then the antianswer may seem to be doubt. If I need help unasking the question, I probably need to listen to the doubts that undo both the answers and the questions. The very thing that can help me—the nudging of doubt toward a deeper exploration—is often something I've demonized and feared. Doubt is the friend of questions, and doubt is the teacher of truth. And really, what are the deepest questions we can ask? And is an answer—the very idea of it is a noun: a person, place, or thing—ever going to be finally adequate? Perhaps *answer* is best understood as *answering*, an active verb, a living, breathing, confusing, active verb?

All of this is to say that if there is only one answer, then it devalues the breadth of questions being asked. I've heard arguments that Jesus can help with mortgage payments, depression, debt, relational breakdown, loneliness, and guilt. Having stories of my own about all of these things, I can say that Jesus certainly helped as much as he harmed, and the influence of the story of Jesus of Nazareth in my life has both aided and ailed maturity at different times. At times I have asked, "What does it mean to be an adult?" Other times I have asked, "What does it mean to have meaning?" Other times I have asked, "What do I do with my loneliness?" Once, my wonderful friend Jenny said to me, "What do I do with all of my rage?" And another time, a four-year-old Zambian boy asked me, "Do you know what fear is?"

Hello to questions that come at odd angles.

♀

There is something reasonably predictable about the story called "The Good Samaritan," as it is often interpreted. Be generous and considerate to those who are in dire circumstances, the message could say. Or, be nice to your neighbor when your neighbor is destitute or dying or bleeding. It's a good message, but there is nothing particularly new about it if read in a certain way. However, if read in another way, there is something entirely undoing in it, because the text undoes question, presumption, entitlement, and agency.

The introduction to the story known as the Good Samaritan is insightful. While the evangelist Luke doesn't always give insider knowledge about the characters engaging Jesus, he does in this instance. An expert in the law, Luke narrates, comes to test Jesus and, to this end, asks a question about how to inherit eternal life.

This always reminds me of Oscar Wilde's *The Importance of Being Earnest*. In this play, called a trivial comedy for serious people, there is a central character, known as Earnest in the country and Jack in the town. Jack is, he believes, his real name, but he likes to have two names so that he can maintain a noble reputation in the country—where he has a young ward, Cecily—while philandering in the town. He becomes engaged to Gwendolen, a woman dear to him. She is enthralled at the engagement, particularly because she has always known that she will marry a man named Earnest. So serious is her desire that she will not marry a man with another name; hence the importance of being Earnest for this man called Jack. Just after their engagement, this twice-named man says to his beloved, "But you don't really mean to say that you couldn't love me if my name wasn't Earnest?"

To which Gwendolen replies, "But your name is Earnest."

Jack comes back with "Yes, I know it is. But supposing it was something else? Do you mean to say you couldn't love me then?"

Gwendolen replies, "Ah! But that is clearly a metaphysical speculation, and like most metaphysical speculations, it has very little reference at all to the actual facts of real life, as we know them."

Gwendolen's glib reply highlights both the truth and the untruth of the situation. The untruth is that the matter is metaphysical. In truth, the matter is entirely pragmatic—the man she is engaged to is, in fact, known as Jack as well as Earnest, so the question of his name has much reference to the facts of real life. The problem is that the facts of his real life are known neither to her nor, as the story reveals, to her fiancé. Oscar Wilde is, at once, revealing both the deception at the heart of disembodied speculation as well as the truth that much of what passes as theory is, in fact, related very much to the facts of life, but obliquely, so as to hide the real motivation.

Hello to the agendas we've managed to hide, even from ourselves.

The man questioning Jesus in Luke is asking a question, a metaphysical speculation, about eternal life. It seems that Jesus understands that a trick is happening, and so he responds with a statement and a question that demonstrates a pearl of Jewish religion. "You know the Torah," Jesus replies. "How do you read it?" Theology speaks of both exegesis and hermeneutics. Exegesis is the study of the written word and hermeneutics is the recognition of the lenses we use to read the words. Here we have both exegesis and hermeneutics. Jesus is drawing out the distinction between knowledge of the inked word and the agenda employed in reading—and acting on—that word. It is as if he's saying, "How does the way you read the text inform the way you act?" The suspicion I have is that if the way you read the text leads you to hate, then you are not reading the text properly. Augustine of Hippo, a man about whom much can be said, put it more elegantly: "Whoever, then, thinks that he understands the Holy Scriptures, or any part of them, but puts such an interpretation on them as does not tend to build up this twofold love of God and our neighbour, does not yet understand them as he ought."

Responding now to Jesus, the teacher of the law offers—although I always imagine he muttered resentfully—an acceptable summation of the law: You must love the Lord your God with all your blah blah blah, to which Jesus replied, "You have answered correctly." The genius of the writer of Luke is that now the heart of the matter emerges. What had begun as a metaphysical speculation is now revealed to be nothing of the sort. In asking questions about eternal life, the teacher of the law had, all the while, been asking about something much more related to himself. Luke expresses it like this: "But the teacher of the law, anxious to justify himself, asked . . ."

Here we have arrived at the nugget, the kernel, the heart of the engagement. The purpose of the exchange was not to talk about eternal life. The exchange was a game centered on the art of self-justification. The man had come to Jesus with a trick question, but Jesus tricked the trickster into answering his own trick question, and when this was revealed the hidden question came to the fore. What was the man's deepest question? I think it was something like "If everybody is my neighbor, then how do I know that I'm good?"

◆

Hello to those I consider beneath me.

◆

Jesus responds with a story, and it is important to understand that Jesus was responding from the heart of a Jewish sensibility. He wasn't saying something alien to the Jewish law or Jewish custom; he was speaking from the heart of the faith that had formed him.

In the Shelter

I've never liked the title "The Good Samaritan" because it seems to imply that the Samaritan in question was an exception—that most of them were not good, but that this one was surprising. The story is well known: A man is going on a journey and on his way is beaten up by robbers who leave him for dead. A religious figure passes him but doesn't aid him, and a second religious figure repeats the actions of the first. A Samaritan, however, comes and aids the man most generously. It is a text that plays on hyperbole—the robbers are all awful, the religious figures are all without compassion, and the only moral hero is the Samaritan. It builds on the understanding that Jews and Samaritans, communities with a common past but a fractured present, would find it difficult to see goodness in each other.

The genius of the text is that here the Jewish man from Nazareth is saying that in order to reconsider neighborliness, we must not only be kind to those in need but be willing to be helped by those from whom help would hurt. Gandalf tried to send Gollum to the Elves for help, but Gollum could never receive help from those fierce Elves with bright eyes. From whom would I reject help? Why would I reject help? Because it hurts to receive help from someone whose moral capacity I have denied. If I receive help from them, then I must ask a new question, I must undo the old questions, and I must revisit the prejudice that considers that help from "them"—no matter who they are—is an exception.

Jesus finished his parable and asked, "Who was the neighbor?" and the man seeking to justify himself answered, "The one who showed him mercy." Jesus then said, "Go and do likewise." I wonder what that imperative was—to go and give help to those who might despise you? Or to go and receive help from those you despise? Both, I assume, and even more.

Hello to the help that'll hurt.

♀

In her essay "Come September," Arundhati Roy wrote, "Writers imagine that they cull stories from the world. I'm beginning to believe that vanity makes them think so. That it's actually the other way around. Stories cull writers from the world. Stories reveal themselves to us. The public narrative, the private narrative—they colonize us. They commission us. They insist on being told. Fiction and nonfiction are only different techniques of story telling." If my life were fiction, I think I'd still write me into the folds of Belfast. I grew up in an ordinary Irish Catholic family—baptism, communion, confession, turning into Satan in the bathroom mirror, the rosary, the priest, the bishop's inspection—but after ten years something new happened. My parents had joined a Catholic charismatic prayer group. My older sister Áine mentioned once that it was annoying how announcements at the prayer group overused the verb *encourage* instead of more direct imperatives. "Can we encourage everybody to be on time?" or "Can we encourage all the mothers in the room to pray for their husbands?" *Encouragement* was a plasterword that bled a lot of orders, it seemed. As a result of this prayer group, much changed. I began to meet Protestants, hitherto an unknown species. "They don't like Mary" is all I knew, and "They think we're wrong." That I would think they were wrong was an assumed expectation. From the age of eleven, I went to Christmas and Easter and summer camps where I was one among a small number of Catholics surrounded by Irish Protestants. They knew Bible verses and could recite whole texts in response to Scripture references being called out. Sword drill, they called it. A leader at the camp would shout out "John Three Sixteen" and twenty clear-voiced Protestants who spoke with what I'd call posh-Irish accents would chime,

> Forgodsolovedtheworldthathegavehisonlysonthat-
> whosoeverwouldbelieveinhimwouldnotperishbut-
> wouldhaveeternallife.

I was intimidated and awed. Who were these people who knew so much? I practiced speaking with a posh accent and quietly asked questions about what "Christ" meant. When someone called out a Scripture reference, they turned to the correct section of their well-read Bibles while I turned crisp unread pages to the index of mine. At night I read frightening stories from the Revised Translation before falling into a complicated sleep.

At these camps, I met wonderful people and fearful people. Most of them were wonderful, but the ones who were fearful are easier to remember. One man taught me my first chords on the guitar, an instrument that I still love almost thirty years later. Another prayed for the gifts of the spirit when I was eleven and I cried because I was frightened and didn't know what to do. A woman, Annette, asked me for a hug and I didn't know what a hug was to give her, and a man saw that I had a wart on my finger and told me that there was a demon in my hand and he prayed for it to be removed. I've never looked at warts the same since. It was a cocktail of devotion and discovery, certainty and chaos.

For my teenage years, I went to Bible camps run by Protestants. Some of them saw me as a project for proselytism, and I learned that not all Christians saw all Christians as Christians. I learned that when asked, "When did you become a Christian?" that neither the answer "*mu*" nor "at my baptism" satisfied, so I—always a child with a yearning for drama—invented before-and-after stories that tickled my whimsy for narrative while, I now realize, concealing little.

Hello to the fictions we tell. They tell us a lot.

◊

At the age of eleven, I was approached by a boy from my class. "Pádraig, are you a homosexual or a homosapien?" he asked, and I knew that there was a proper answer to this trick question. I knew that I was supposed to answer yes to one, and no to the other. I didn't really know what homosexual meant, but I knew what got you called a faggot. I thought I had the right answer, and by this I knew I didn't mean the true answer, just the right one for the circumstance—and I answered, confidently, "I am a homosexual." I won't forget what came afterward. Small boys bruise in the ego and the skin.

Hello to the stories of survival.

I remember talking to my friend Jeff, and he said, "Do you remember when you realized, simultaneously, what a faggot was and that you're not supposed to tell anybody?" We were both in our thirties when we talked about this, and his assumption of a shared narrative of growing up gay in the Ireland of the 1980s was a relief.

For my teenage years, I quietly searched for information about being gay. At youth festivals run by the Anglican Church, I slipped into the back of seminars talking about "struggling with a homosexual orientation" and learned vocabulary from speakers who, it later turned out, didn't even believe their own rhetoric. They were just doing what they thought they needed to do to survive. I learned that lust was a demon, just like warts, but deeper and more dangerous. I learned to hate arousal and denounce attraction. I learned a syntax of sex that dissected humanity into what was safe and what was sinful. Jesus was a comfort for the sorrowful, but his swordy tongue was a fearful thing indeed. I read the book of Revelation and shut it tight. I read the Gospels and feared the world to come. I read Paul and learned to lie, and I read about burdens and shoulders and yokes and shared weights and hung on to threads of consolation. I wrote coded poetry and memorized Elvish. Lothlórien, a woodland home of Elves, is called, in the language of Ents, "Land of the Valley of Singing Gold." I didn't know why it moved me so much, but it did.

I searched for answers about why I might be gay. There were books on shelves in church shops about the causes and cures of homosexuality, and I lied when friends asked me what books I was reading. I abandoned fiction and poetry for a few years until it felt like my faith abandoned me, and I clawed my way back to words using the only thing that worked: fiction and poetry and the love of language. There, I discovered something more true than the half-truths I'd stung myself with.

Hello to what we cannot know

Once, I heard about a priest who was sympathetic to gay people. I wrote him a letter, and it was a long letter, ten pages of typed narrative. He wrote back and suggested we meet. He had enjoyed the letter, he said, although he was confused. "What if you could find out about what made you gay?" he said. "Would it change anything?" He had a point. The story I'd inherited said that being gay was a result of neglect, or overattention, or identification with one parent, or nonidentification with the other. It was pathetic psychology from blow-up armchairs and had neither weight nor substance but was legion in impact. It was what I have begun to describe as moral ideology. We don't know what the truth is, but we know what we need our answer to be. And the answer is this, so therefore you're wrong. Bad endings require bad beginnings, and if an education in poetry and mathematics has taught me anything, it's that elegance and form reveal truth and meaning. Predetermined answers lead to lazy thinking.

Hello to the desperate search for certainty.

What was I searching for? These days, I think I was searching for the possibility of love. The possibility of being loved. Even a dream would have been nice. Once, I was walking around a supermarket, and a song came on the radio. It was "Country Roads" by John Denver. I'd learned that song climbing a mountain as a child with my dad and some of his friends. One of them, a lovely woman named Bríd, taught me the words on the way down the mountain, and I've not forgotten them since. Walking around the supermarket, I found myself thinking, "I'd love to be in love so I could sing this song for a boyfriend."

It was a small conversion. It converted me because I was surprised by the ordinariness of the desire. This was not the gay agenda I'd been taught about by those who invented an agenda to prove the point they needed to prove. The gay agenda was trying to undermine love, trying to undermine family, trying to undermine morality and subjectivity and truth and God and Jesus, Mary, and Joseph.

But here I was, crying in the aisle of a supermarket because I had just surprised myself by dreaming of the possibility of sharing love.

Hello to the surprise of the ordinary.

Hello to the aisle of a supermarket.

Hello to the lovely question.

♀

Once, during a phone conversation, a friend asked me what I was reading and I decided to tell the truth. "A book about homosexuality," I said, as lightly as I could. She said, "I'm coming to see you this weekend," then she drove a hundred miles and said, "I'm taking you book shopping." I had little money, but she stood me in front of a bookshelf in the largest bookshop in Dublin and said, "Choose one, and you're paying." I bought two: one about theology and one about a life. *Becoming a Man: Half a Life Story* by Paul Monette was a book that I loved and read and reread and carried with me throughout a nomadic decade. There was one paragraph I could recite by heart. Monette was in the middle of a summer trip around Europe and had met an old school friend in Italy: "I remember this very specific moment when all those guards came down. We'd taken the ferry to Capri, and after the Blue Grotto tour Francis and I found ourselves swimming naked off a rock below the cliffs of Tiberius' villa. As we paddled back and forth in the cobalt water, I suddenly felt an overwhelming need to tell him the truth. Thought I would die of the pretense if I had to endure it a moment longer." Reading somebody else's life was a salve to the life that I thought I could never live. Curiously, Monette criticized himself for "living my life of a book instead of a person," and his caution about using literature as a cell rang true to my usage of religion. Time to begin asking a different question, I began to realize. Instead of answering, "I'm a heterosexual who struggles with a homosexual orientation," I began to favor a more simple syntax. "I'm gay," I began saying to myself, whispering it when walking along roads by myself. I took a lot of long walks, usually along Griffith Avenue. At the time—and maybe still—it was Europe's longest treelined avenue and made for good walks, whatever the weather.

Rather than "How did I develop homosexuality?" as if it were a disease or a symptom, I began to ask a different question. I didn't even know the question that I needed to ask, but it needed to be different, because the answer I was beginning to live was an answer that opened itself to life. The question was, I think, "How can I live my life without resentment?" and it suggested an answer less to do with obligation and more to do with choice and freedom and conscience and respect given and respect received.

In the Shelter

Of course, there was curiosity about sex. How could there not be? As a seventeen-year-old, I had once seen a scene in a film where a man got into bed with another man. It wasn't erotic, it was loving and ordinary. I was astonished but changed the channel quickly when I heard the door open. A few years later, I heard a Bible teacher say that "homosexuality is purely about lust, that's all. It's nothing more complex than a lustful life." I was very frightened at the time, and pretty naive, but I remember writing in my notebook, "He hasn't a damned clue." I was shocked at what I wrote.

Hello to certainty.

The beloved Nuala O'Faolain was an Irish commentator who wrote editorials for the *Irish Times* for much of the 1990s. In her first published collection, she wrote, "There will be many, many men in Ireland who will never in their lives be held in a passionate embrace, because heterosexual bigotry has forced them into darkness." I had found her book *Are You Somebody?* in a secondhand bookshop on a weekend trip to the Dingle gaeltacht (Irish-speaking region) with my dad. I loved her prose, her feminism, her scalpel-sharp syntax, her analysis of religion, Ireland, politics, and conflict. I knew she wouldn't like my religion, but I always felt that her generosity was deeper than her opinions. Shortly before she died in 2008, in an interview with the journalist—and her friend—Marian Finucane,

Hello to what we cannot know

Nuala said, "As soon as I heard I was going to die, the goodness went from life." I grieved at this story. She, through her humor, truth telling, and exploration of the world, had given me so much goodness. Hers was a lonely vocation, and one she lived truthfully, to bear witness to Ireland, and she did it so well. Through her truth telling, she helped me tell some truths to myself and ask some new questions.

Hello to the voice of wisdom, the voice of blessed memory.

♀

Toward the end of the Gospel of John, a resurrection narrative is recorded. Mary of Magdala has gone to the tomb of Jesus. She had gone initially with Peter and the other disciple, the one Jesus loved, but they returned to their homes. Mary stayed weeping outside the tombs, and there she encountered a man she did not recognize. She assumed he was the gardener. He asked her why she was weeping and for whom she was looking. This, the Gospel that steals the story that begins with *B*, is continuing on the Edenic motif in its structure and telling. The Gospel opened with a retelling of the seven days, at the culmination of which was a wedding, a celebration, and an abundance of good wine. Here, at the end, is a person crying in the garden, and she meets someone she does not recognize.

Mary is the soul of the world, returned into the garden of creation but unsure of how to greet the characters there. The gardener, shrouded in a sunhat and skin, says to her, "Mary." It is only here, in hearing her name spoken, that she sees where she could not previously see, and she sees that the gardener is the Gardener, and that the body is the Body and that what was dead is now beyond death.

And then he says the most curious thing: "*Do not cling to me.*"

What a strange thing to say. They have found each other, and she, in the reciprocality of her name, has perceived God where before she only saw labor, and she is told not to cling. Much can be made of the exchange. The verb for "cling" here is *haptō*, meaning to touch, grasp, or ignite. Were I to meet someone in this circumstance, I would want to touch them to see if they burst, and then, if they didn't, to cling, and grasp, and keep. As with all texts, the reading of the meaning can vary. I like to think that it was wisdom Jesus was giving Mary, not correction. Don't think that you can hold on to me: the point isn't to grasp, the point is to do. And do what? Well, that's the question.

Language, language, language. It's all we've got. It isn't final, but it's not a bad start. St. Jerome, the fourth-century man from Dalmatia who is credited with assembling the corpus of the New Testament as we know it today, said, "No similitude can be implied of God without implying an even greater dissimilitude," which is to say, when you think you've found a way to speak about God, you have also found a way to unspeak about God. Avivah Zornberg puts it a different way when she says that in order to write words about God we have to recognize that any words about God will be limited, simply because no word is big enough. It's as if she's implying that God may be glad when we perceive the limitations in the holy words—these limitations don't undo the God behind the text, they just undo the language used. Even that sentence is limited—how can we say that God is glad? But to undo language is not the final point: the point is to play with it, and in play, *glad* is a good word. Play can imply winning, but play can also imply playing.

○

The Zulus have it right, though, in one of their names for God. They call God *uNkulunkulu*, translating loosely as "Big-Big." When I heard that, I wondered at the genius who began to speak of the unnameable in such a way, and then I thought of my friend Emma, a farmer from Ireland who lives in Portugal with her wife, Bárbara. She writes letters and asks for prayers to The Bigness. One time, we talked about it, and she said that The Bigness is also The Smallness and that each can hold the other.

Hello to the bigness in the smallness.

○

All of this sounds suspiciously like what I was taught to fear. I was taught to fear questions and I was taught to fear doubt. "*Is doimhin é poll an amhrais,*" the old saying says in Irish—deep is the hole of doubt. And perhaps that's where the nightmares of caves came from. But there is much to be learned from digging, and there is more to Moria than the Balrog and its wrath. There are also diamonds and books and caverns filled with lights that light themselves.

In the Shelter

Fortunately, I had learned to like doubt early on. My mother told me that St. Thérèse had, in the last few days of her life, found herself in the pit of despair because of the absolute lack of any consolation or hope. She, according to the story I remember my mother telling me, died in this state, and it was her vocation to die in this state. It seemed a cruel God who'd concoct such a plan, but it helped me see something bigger than doubt. I'm pretty sure this story isn't true, but that doesn't matter; it worked. Later on, when I was introduced to a faith language that held more sway for certainty, I was, for a while, tempted by the illusion of final certainty, but that temptation fell away before too long. I had my mother's story. And I had met too many generous people who fell outside the borders of the realms of the righteous to be too long convinced by rhetoric that categorized before it asked. I was aided by Stewart Henderson, who, in his poem "I Believe," wrote,

> I believe propaganda is ideological Valium.
> Propagandists are mynah birds,
> excellent mimics
> But don't expect them to say anything original.
> I believe in doubt
> I believe doubt is a process of saying
> "Excuse me, I have a question."
> Propagandists hate questions
> and in so doing
> detest art.
> I believe in art.

Hello to what we cannot know

That time that everything fell apart, that time when I thought the only way to go forward was to leave God behind—of all places to go, I went to Taizé, a monastery. I know, it's as transparent as my gay friend who went to a beach full of handsome men in Speedos to pray about being celibate. But I went to a monastery in an attempt to say goodbye to God. I brought poetry, theology, and fiction, good companions for every journey. The fiction held me, the poetry read me, and, little by little, the theology started to sound different. I said goodbye to some things, but I said hello to doubt, questions, and prayer.

Hello to the uncertain walk of faith.

Narrative Theology # 2

I used to need to know
the end of every story
but these days I only
need the start to get me going.

God is the crack
where the story begins.
We are the crack
where the story gets interesting.

We are the choice of
where to begin—
the person going out?
the stranger coming in?

God is the fracture,
and the ache in your voice,
God is the story
flavored with choice.

God is the pillar of salt
full of pity
accusing God
for the sulfurous city.

God is the woman who bleeds
and who touches.
We are the story
of courage or blushes.

God is the story
of whatever works.
God is the twist at the end
and the quirks.

We are the start,
and we're at the center,
we are the characters,
narrators, inventors.

God is the bit
that we can't explain—
maybe the healing
maybe the pain.

We are the bit
that God can't explain—
maybe the harmony
maybe the strain.

God is the plot,
and we are the writers,

the story of winners
and the story of fighters,

the story of love,
and the story of rupture,
the story of stories,
the story without structure.

6

Hello to the body

I've been undone by bodily self-consciousness since I was a child. I remember when it started—I was at a summer camp with other children and somebody came up to me and said, "You've got a long chin." I didn't entirely know what they meant by that, but I remember the process of staring in the mirror trying to measure my chin in comparison with other parts of my face. Then somebody told me I had an unusually shaped head, and then somebody told me I had long legs. Then puberty started and school showers were a displaying of the unloved body and it seemed that each year brought a new layer of self-consciousness, a new focus on another part of the body that was different from what I could see in others. I knew I was gay—by this stage I'd begun whispering "I am one of them" to myself when nobody else was at home—and that seemed to compound the self-consciousness.

I also had a particular friend. I was going to write a peculiar friend, but that wouldn't have done him justice. However, he was peculiar in the way he practiced the project of convincing me that I was ugly. Between his peculiar project and the questions about the face, the chin, the body, the self that divides its self from the self, a small chaos was opened.

One day, when I was fifteen, I looked in the mirror and saw the things that I had learned were disproportionate, or unusual, or laughable. I thought, "If I can say the worst thing to myself, then it won't hurt as much if others say it." So I said it.

I am ugly.

Hello.

A good-looking friend once said that she hated her elbows, and I found myself looking at her with incomprehension. Of all the things to dislike about your body, I had never considered elbows to be a focus of attention. It was a mild relief, I suppose, and not because it indicated that the beautiful also suffer, but because it was an easy way to realize the selfishness of self-consciousness. I didn't care about my friend's elbows, and even if they had been as ugly as her own despair indicated, I liked her because of her wit, her laugh, her small rebellions, and her sharp tongue. I began to look around at other people I loved and admired and realized that, were I to imagine myself in their bodies, I'd find all measures of things to hate: teeth; ears; small eyes; strange hands; irritating laughs; voices too high, too low; height. I wondered whether women made jokes to each other about the sizes of their breasts in the way that men did about the size of their penises and I wondered if the measure of gender is size or—I began to dare—confidence in your own very self.

Hello to the body. It has much to tell us.

Hello to the body

Carol Ann Duffy writes a poem of Pilate's wife, who, when Jesus of Nazareth entered Jerusalem, crept out with her maid to see this strange man:

> His face? Ugly. Talented.
> He looked at me. I mean he looked at *me*. My God.
> His eyes were to die for. Then he was gone,
> His rough men shouldering a pathway to the gates.

I love the side-by-side descriptions of the imagined face of Jesus. Ugly. Talented. These descriptors are neither contradictions nor oxymorons. Once a person came to me at Greenbelt, my favorite festival in the world. She said, "When I first saw you speak in the distance, I thought you were beautiful. Then I came closer and I realized that you're not." At this stage, I was already rehearsing her accent, knowing this would be a story I'd get mileage from. She then said, "But now we've spoken with each other for a while, I realize that you are beautiful—on the inside." I believe she meant it as a compliment, and while at the time I was bewildered at her unreflective self-confidence, I suppose that now I see it as a strange compliment, and one that, ultimately, I would hope is true. Carol Ann Duffy's poem imagines what it's like to be held in the gaze of someone whose face is not extraordinary, but with whom an encounter is measured by something other than how their face rates. Pilate's wife, in this poem, sees a face that's quickly characterized, but ultimately she herself feels like she is the one being gazed upon, in a small moment. Do we ever really see others, I wonder? Or do we usually see something of ourselves in faces that we look at? We see whether we are more or less beautiful than they.

Hello to the eyes, and to the eyes that look, and the eyes that look back.

Hello to the gaze.

At a storytelling evening in Belfast—a monthly evening that my partner and I started a few years ago—the theme was "Bodies." We had nine people telling true stories about bodies, and two of the offerings that evening described life-drawing classes where, with charcoal and paper, artists drew images of the nude model in front of them. One of the storytellers spoke of her first experience drawing a model. The model was a woman in her late forties who was calm and ordinary. When the time came for the class to draw, the model disrobed and took a pose. The storyteller spoke of what a delight it was to draw a person whose body told a story: stretchmarks and bodybumps; a body inhabited, a body told and held. The storyteller said that all the drawings of the model that night were full of character because the subject owned and knew—and probably loved—her body so well. At another class, a life model came in whose body was almost perfect, but whose poses told a story of anxiety and self-consciousness, and the artists' works that night—even the most talented—were hesitant and without life.

Hello to the body

During a particularly long period of self-consciousness, I was taking a long walk. As I was walking, I noticed somebody coming toward me from the other direction. I ached as I watched him because his walk told a story of inhabiting his own body. As I came closer, I realized that I knew him. It was Jimmy, a man generous and good and ordinary. His walk told a story of inhabiting his body with the vernacular of ease. It seems that to live well with your own body is to find yourself eavesdropping into a quiet conversation inside yourself. For some, this seems to have been easy. For others it has been a long labor, and for still others it's a torture.

"Hope has two lovely daughters," Augustine of Hippo is credited with saying, "anger and courage. Anger at the way things are and courage to change them." I think that if the body has two wise daughters, then they are loneliness and vulnerability. Loneliness in order to face your true self and vulnerability enough to tell the story to others. The cruelty of our half-lived lives is a false story of connection based on appearance and comparison, and such connections are parasitic on human community. Those connections glue people together with fear and tell some that they are enough for themselves, that their loneliness and vulnerability are abated. When I was a school chaplain, a young person once wrote a prayer for our end-of-day service. He wrote it, he read it out, and then he threw it in the bin. I fished it out and framed it and hung it on my wall. I do not know what other prayer to pray:

In the Shelter

Dear God.
Thank you for putting me on this earth
but people can get lonely
and I don't like people being lonely
cause sometimes I am
and it's not a good feeling.
So I'd like you to pair them up
with someone who is ~~not~~ lonely
if you can.
Amen.

☹ could be ☺.

He read the prayer with such simple truth that I thought I would break. The prayer had a picture at the end of a sad face covered by a raincloud and a happy face in the middle of a sun. Sad could be happy, I understand this to say, or rainy could be sunny. There is such humble conditionality in the structure of the prayer. I don't know if I've ever heard more beautiful usage of the three words *If you can*. It's as if he understood that there are limits to what God can do but that there's no harm in asking.

When I started studying theology, I was introduced to the idea of redaction criticism, the skill of discovering how the texts that we now accept as a literary whole may be the product of decades of editing, with changes, additions, and extractions having happened. In redaction criticism, the scholar asks why Luke tells the story of John the Baptist differently to Mark, when it is assumed that Luke had access to the text of Mark. Redaction critics see the layers of edits within a text and give great value to the meaning behind edits. When I met this twelve-year-old and heard his prayer, I wondered at the ~~not~~. Clearly he had initially written the line as "So I'd like you to pair them up with some-one who is not lonely, if you can," but later on returned and made the "not" a "~~not~~."

Hello to loneliness.

What does loneliness have to do with the body? I think that the relationship with the body is close to the relationship with our selves. And when we are alone, when we are invited into a space where comparison with others—whether that leads to a sense of superiority or inferiority—is removed, then there are questions we must ask ourselves. When I was fifteen I woke up in the middle of the night, reached for some paper, and wrote, in the dark, a short poem that comforted me once I had woken up:

> And who are you
> when you're alone
> in the dark
> when you're at home?

It has enough predictable teenage angst in it to be ignorable but, I think, it was some kind of wisdom—the wisdom that prompted me toward working out my relationship with my body based on a relationship with myself, not on any relationships of comparison. Friendship with your body should be based not on comparison but on something more solitary. Friendship with others should be based on need and generosity, not dominance.

♀

Luke's Gospel contains a story that is loved by many, and all too often only told to children. Luke has been directing Jesus back to Jerusalem for almost ten chapters, and the tension is building. The readers are being invited into the drama of the question: What will happen when Jesus reaches the city? Just before Jesus arrives in Jerusalem, he passes through Jericho—geography is merely a tool, not a burden for the writer—and has already passed through when he notices a small man in a sycamore tree.

Ken Bailey makes a convincing argument about the placing of the tree. The sycamore, because of its wide canopy, was understood to be a way in which the sins of one household could be transferred to another household because the sins could travel under a shared canopy of leaves and branches. So in order to avoid one household being tainted with the wrongdoings of another, such wide-spreading trees were required to be planted outside the city bounds. So Zacchaeus, the small man reputed to have big pockets, runs to the sin-spreading tree and climbs into it. He had tried to see through the crowd but he couldn't, so now he, like a child, climbs a tree.

Jesus stops, and looks up, and tells Zacchaeus to come down, because he is to stay at his house that night, and then the people grumble. It's not a surprise that it's a story used for children, as it lends itself to slapstick caricatures. But it's a story about stature, about using power to rise above your contemporaries, about a sense of betrayal, about taxes, about unfair taxes, and about how sometimes the privileged are the victims of their own measures. The narrator of the text never calls Zacchaeus particularly greedy; it's the other Jericho residents who grumble, and who knows? Maybe Zacchaeus was just lucky, not corrupt. It's a story about a man and his body, and how compensation for stature through elevated status is eventually unsatisfactory. When Jesus looks up, he says, "Come down." It's a gorgeous play of theological topography. Jesus, whose long story of arrival at Jerusalem seems almost to be at an end, delays his arrival one more night. He imposes himself with easy self-invitation on the generosity of a man whose reputation is less than generous.

It is as if the text is telling a story of overcompensation for an uneasy relationship with masculinity's relationship with size. Size of body and size of influence. Where Zacchaeus saw his redemption through social ascension, Jesus calls him down to the level of generosity. It was a generosity that began with a night of hospitality, and—if Zacchaeus is to be believed—continued.

So loneliness has a lovely son: confidence. And confidence has a loving brother: generosity. And they are shown in both the language and gesture of the body.

Hello to the sons and daughters of loneliness.

◉

I have a friend—Jim—who is not a small man. Jim describes himself as a "big boy," and his generosity is large and wonderful. Jim is a fan of the Icelandic band Sigur Rós, and a number of years ago he bought two expensive tickets for a gig they were playing in England. One ticket for him and one for a friend who had longed to see the band play. Sigur Rós play loud music; they sometimes sing in a language—Hopelandic—that they've made up. Jim and his friend went to the concert and it was everything they hoped it would be—big music, soaring layers of harmonic scream, Icelandic and Hopelandic lyrics, pure noise that shakes and lifts and does and undoes you.

Jim, when he was telling me the story, said, "If you think I'm big, my mate is bigger." And he spoke of how, halfway through the concert, when the layers of music were so loud and pure and clear that they'd break your heart, a brass band walked through the crowd.

These were small Icelandic boys with eyes as bright as their buttons and they had red uniforms like little soldiers. The music was building and right through the crowd these boys walked with their trombones and tubas, trumpets and timpani. Jim's mate was so moved by the marching band that he started to cry for the sheer delight of the brass sight and sound of it. Jim, who calls himself a softie, is incapable of allowing anybody to cry alone, and so he started to cry himself. They stood there, two big English men, crying with their arms around each other. Then, to their surprise and satisfaction, another man, a stranger standing behind them wearing an Iron Maiden T-shirt—himself also big—came up and wrapped them both in his own two thick manly arms and the trinity of big English men stood there and wept with joy at the sight of small boys from the North Atlantic playing bright tunes on brass instruments.

Hello to the body

This is a story about size and men. This is a story about men and our emotions. This is a story about strangers and strangeness and loneliness and tears and music and small boys' games and big boys' bodies. It is a story too about the generous gesture. This is a story about men and our bodies, or, at least, it could be.

Hello to the story of men and our bodies.

♀

In the field of Cormallen, Frodo and Sam are being praised for their work in destroying the ring of power. When all had seemed lost, Sam had comforted Frodo with a little imagination. He had said that at some point a song would be sung that would praise their lonely journey. It was a nice idea at the time, but Frodo was so burdened that he couldn't even imagine it. Now, their task complete, they are in a field and somebody has said, "Praise them with great praise!" and a minstrel comes and sings a song of Frodo of the Nine Fingers and the Ring of Doom:

> And when Sam heard that he laughed aloud for sheer
> delight, and he stood up and cried: "O great glory
> and splendour! And all my wishes have come true!" And
> then he wept. And all the host laughed and wept,
> and in the midst of their merriment and tears the clear
> voice of the minstrel rose like silver and gold, and all
> men were hushed. And he sang to them, now in the
> Elven-tongue, now in the speech of the west, until

> their hearts, wounded with sweet words, overflowed,
> and their joy was like swords, and they passed in
> thought out to regions where pain and delight flow
> together and tears are the very wine of blessedness.

Hello to knowing our body through surviving with others.

♦

The Ireland I grew up in was not an Ireland that knew much about hugging. Maybe it was particularly true for Irish boys; I don't know whether it was different for girls. One Irish way of saying "hug" is *duine a theannadh le do chroí*—to squeeze somebody with your heart. It's lovely but I never knew it. That first time I was asked for a hug and I got one—even though I didn't know I had one to either give or take—I found myself thinking, "So this is what arms are for."

When I think of that time, I now think of it together with Michael Ondaatje's beautiful poem "Bearhug." In it, Ondaatje tells of his small son, Griffin, calling for his dad to come in and kiss him goodnight. Ondaatje finishes one piece of work, then another, and then another, and when finally he gets to the room, he finds that Griffin has been standing there with arms stretched out, grinning:

> This is the hug which collects
> all his small bones and his warm neck against me.
> The thin tough body under the pyjamas
> locks to me like a magnet of blood.

Hello to the body

> How long was he standing there
> like that, before I came?

To live in the body is to be a body. I can only speak as a person with the body of a man, and as a man. I know that there is a deeper language of the manbody than the language of prowess or domination. It is the language of confidence, of gesture, of holding and generosity.

Hello to being a body with other bodies.

When Zacchaeus made his announcement about returning monies to anybody he'd stolen from or cheated—and I always imagine this statement to have been made in the midst of a generous party—Jesus makes an extraordinary statement. He says, "Today salvation has come to this house, because he too is a son of Abraham." Zacchaeus has been working as a tax collector for an occupying force. The Romans were only the latest in a long line of forces that flexed their muscles in Judea. There had been the Assyrians, the Babylonians, the Persians, the Greeks, and now the Romans. And so, to make a collusive living out of tax collecting for an unwelcome army would have been a complicated thing indeed.

"He's no son of Abraham," I imagine people said.

Hello to betrayal.

To collude with the unwelcome army is to abdicate your identity. Locations all around the world have words for this role. *Tout* is the word in Ireland that connotes "traitor," "informant," "snake in the grass." It's an insult and it's a danger. So Jesus's words, generous words that build on a generous response to a generous demand, seem to go against this tendency of ours to disinherit those we think have betrayed us. He honors membership in a society. He doesn't say, "This man *now* is a Son of Abraham, *again*"; he says, "This man too is a Son of Abraham." It is a complicated thing to share identity.

♀

The body can tell truth to us. Years ago, somebody snapped a photograph at a farewell party. I had been in a job for a few years and was now going away. My working relationship with my boss had not always been easy; my questions, apparently, had the scent of rebellion, and as we all know, rebellion is as the sin of witchcraft. Nonetheless, despite our different approaches to practically everything, there was affection between my boss and me. At the farewell party, we were saying goodbye and going in for a hug. We were about to squeeze each other with our hearts when somebody snapped that photograph and, months later, sent it to me. On my face is a look of pure bewilderment. It is as if I am looking at my old boss with a look of incomprehension. "What are you?" I might be saying, or "I come in peace; do you?" The look on my face tells almost the whole story of our working relationship, caught between human connection and mutual incomprehension. I showed the photo to a friend of mine and she laughed and said, "Oh, the body doesn't lie."

Hello to the truths that the body tells.

Hello to the body

In an Ethics class, I learned that the body has integrity, but that one of the exceptions to maintaining the integrity of the body—or, to be surface level about it, the integrity of skin—is surgery. Surgery, my teacher taught, is an ethically acceptable exception to the otherwise important principle that the skin should not be violated by being cut open. A few weeks later, I visited a friend in the hospital. He'd had a serious blood clot removed and had been sliced open from behind his knee to his groin. While invasive, he had been assured that the surgery had every likelihood of success, and so he had tried to calm himself as he prepared for the operation. It was a successful operation, but the day after the surgery, he told me, he found himself crying uncontrollably because of the sense in his body that other people's hands had been under his skin. He said he felt invaded. Another friend of mine, when going for surgery, said she wasn't looking forward to the mutilation of the scalpel. It is in moments like this that the distinction between body and soul becomes more oblique. I am a body and I am a soul. When the body is sliced, it is more than skin deep. And, of course, surgery is done to maintain the body's integrity, not to deplete it. Even the help hurts.

Hello to the truths that the body protects.

♀

I know somebody—and for the purposes of the story, we can understand this someone to be me—who finds it easy to buy clothes when the shape of the body matches the idea of the body. So when I feel like I've got some weight to lose, I find it difficult to clothe the body in things of value. I know that I am not alone in this. I know that this is a mild story. What is the truth that the body is trying to tell here? I don't know—the truth that hostility toward something rarely made much of a difference; the truth that self-health is wiser than self-hate; the truth that certain rewards can be their own oppression, even in the midst of the good idea of weight loss.

♦

The body tells many truths—I am tired, I am sick, I am in need of healing, I am in need of health, I am in need of touch—but I am also conscious that the first truth that is read from the body is often the truth of its sex. A friend gives birth to a baby and we ask, "What is it?" If this is the first query we have—and it is usually the first question I ask—then what truth does that tell about us? Is there ever the possibility that the truth sought could be both wrong and oppressive? Given the truth and accessible public stories of people who are transgender, genderqueer, or intersex, it seems without doubt that we all know people who have told a gendered story about their newborn that, in time, will not be true. The real true story can take a long time to tell because it first needs to be whispered, and often only with brave measures to ensure safety can the real truth of the body be told out loud.

Hello to the brave truths of the body, told aloud or told alone.

I do not know this story because it has never been my story. I was the boy who liked colors and fabrics and gymnastics and was called a faggot before I knew what a faggot was. But I always knew I was a boy even though there didn't seem to be many other boys like me when I was growing up. Other people too always knew they were boys even though their doctors and their families, their structures and their strictures, told them a different story. Their doctors and families told them one thing, but for as long as they can remember, they and their bodies knew the truer truth. The body knows its own truth, and it is often unrelenting.

I sat next to a man during a church service last year, and when the time came for people to call out items to be included in a list of prayers, he asked for the group to pray for him because his uterus was in trouble. It was duly written down and he enjoyed the look of surprise I gave him. We'd only known each other a few weeks, and we hadn't discussed sex or gender identities yet. Over coffee I said, "Your prayer request was filled with new information," and he said, "Oh, I'm intersex, I was born with most sex organs. I love my uterus. Everybody needs one."

A woman nearby said, "I'd happily get rid of mine," and my friend said, "Love your uterus" and winked.

This is a story of the truth of the body. While I've been typing it, my computer program repeatedly changes "intersex" to "interest," another way in which our machines reveal us. People whose sex identity doesn't fit into binary categories—or people whose sex identity has undergone a transformation, or a journey, or a change, or public comment—are repeatedly barraged with questions that demonstrate interest in their genitals, exchanges that are rarely reciprocal. I do not know what it is like to have the feeling that my body lies to the world about what I know the truth to be. To live well, I must believe the truth that others tell, especially when they have been forced into the habit of being habitually unbelieved.

Hello to the unbelievable body.

♀

The book of Acts contains a story of belief. The apostle Philip is—supernaturally, it seems—instructed to go to a certain road between Jerusalem and Gaza, a wilderness road, the text tells us, an uninhabited place, a barren place. Once there, Philip, whose ear hears many whisperings of the Almighty that day, is told to join a passing chariot, and so he runs to it. Inside the chariot is a man, an Ethiopian eunuch, a court official of the Queen of the Ethiopians, a man in charge of the entire treasury of her majesty. This Ethiopian man had gone to Jerusalem to worship and was now returning to his home territory. Luke, who is the author of Acts, writes that Philip overheard the Ethiopian reading a text aloud, and offered interpretative help. But I always think that the story is about something much more akin to mutual conversion.

The Ethiopian man—usually called "the eunuch" in both Acts and other writings—is reading a text from the Hebrew book of Isaiah. The text he is reading is this:

> Like a sheep he was led to the slaughter,
>   and like a lamb before its shearer is silent,
>   so he opens not his mouth.
> In his humiliation justice was denied him.

Hello to the body

> Who can describe his generation?
> For his life is taken away from the earth.

What an appropriate text for a man who has had the sharp shears of a castrator used against him to be reading. Even the location—a barren place—corresponds with his experience; it is like geographic pathetic fallacy. His own justice was, certainly, denied him, and his inheritance, his generations of children, was taken away from him. No wonder the Ethiopian man asked Philip, "About whom, I ask you, does the prophet say this, about himself or about someone else?" Philip begins to speak of Jesus, but I always wonder if the Ethiopian man wondered if there was the possibility that somebody like him could be included in a sacred text. Somebody who is known by public knowledge—and ensuing gendered judgment—of his genital embodiment.

Hello to the things about our body that do not define us.

To be known as "the eunuch" is a cruel and limited eponymy. He, as a eunuch, is identified and named by what he is deemed not to have. So he's landed on the text that speaks of innocence and sharp knives, humiliation, justice, and stolen generations. Philip speaks of Jesus, and it is notable that while the text preserves the direct speech of the Ethiopian, it records nothing of the actual words of Philip, merely detailing briefly his general themes. The directly reported words of the Ethiopian are clearly important.

Having heard Philip's explanation of the meaning of the text, the Ethiopian man asks, "What is to prevent me from being baptized?" These are early days. If Philip were to tell one truth, he would have had to have said, "Everything. Absolutely everything." And then Philip could have quoted Deuteronomy: "No one whose testicles are crushed or whose penis is cut off shall be admitted to the assembly of the Lord." But there was another truth within the tradition of Philip that he showed then:

> To the eunuchs who keep my sabbaths,
> who choose the things that please me
> and hold fast my covenant,
> I will give, in my house and within my walls,
> a monument and a name
> better than sons and daughters;
> I will give them an everlasting name
> that shall not be cut off. (Isaiah 56:4–5)

Given the option of using the religious tradition for exclusion or hoping in the promise of religious inclusion, Philip acted on the latter.

Hello to privilege. Hello to examining your privilege. Hello to conversion.

Philip baptized the Ethiopian man—a moving scene that also moved Rembrandt—and then Philip was snatched away by the spirit of God and found himself at a seaport, Azotus. There, he proclaimed the good news. I wonder what the good news was. I hope it was "I just met a man from Ethiopia who, even though he was excluded, included himself." I read this story understanding that the main beneficiary of the exchange was Philip who, in the presence of someone whose body had been mutilated at another's behest, found himself moved toward the generous and inclusive rather than the turgid and tense. I once led a retreat during which the participants gave each other hand massages. It was a simple gesture, safe, because we each sat on opposite sides of tables. Intimate too—hands can be as sexual as they are practical. After the short exercise, a woman told us that nobody had touched her hands since she had undergone a gender transition some years previously. She shared her story with us with bravery and courage, telling the truth of the impact of isolation and rejection.

Hello to the lonely story of touch.

In Mark's Gospel there is a woman who is keen to touch, but to touch privately. She has heard of Jesus and has suffered much at the hands of many doctors because of chronic bleeding. It seems that she had money at one point because now she has none; she's spent it on doctors and is none the better for her spending. In fact, she's worse. The reader of this text is brought into the privacy of her own world because for a while, at least, none of the other characters in the text know of this woman's existence. It is just her and us, and we are creeping through a jungle of bodies, as she pushes hip and thigh and torso aside to touch the cloth covering the body of a man who might help. She only wants to touch his clothes, not his person; she perhaps wants to leave as unnoticed as she has entered. Some scholars argue that the woman not only was considered unclean in herself but also was bringing uncleanliness to all she touched. Other scholars disagree, saying that everybody understood that nobody measured up to the measures of cleanliness. What is clear, though, is that she enters in claustral cover.

In the Shelter

As she manages to touch the clothes of Jesus, the text weaves a bodystory. *Her* hemorrhage stopped and *she* feels in *her body* that *she* is free of *her* flogging. We are brought into the quiet, private center of her life through this repeated emphasis. The usage of *flogging*, often translated as "disease," is notable, because flogging is done *to* you by another. Her experience of her own body was akin to being flogged. Why was this? Perhaps because her physical impairment was one thing, but the public comment about it was another. Predatory discussion of a body's ability is a disabling torture.

Jesus turns around, having felt in his own body that something had happened, and asks the urgent question, even at the disbelief of his followers. "You're asking who touched you?" they might have said. "Everybody is touching you. We're pushing through a crowd." But there is touch and there is touch, we all know that.

♥

I was once standing on an escalator in Melbourne ascending from the underground train system. Lots of people were pushing past, so I was being jostled, but then—and I can still feel it—a woman placed her hand on my arm. I turned around and she said, "It'd be easier if you stood over to the other side of the escalator." She had a lovely voice, and a manner that seemed to give a window into a life well lived and well liked. Her touch, her hand on my arm, was filled with warmth. An Irish word for warmth is *croíúil*. The first part of this, *croí*, means "heart." The second, *úil*, is a suffix that is often used to turn a noun into an adjective, with the adjective having the characteristic of being like, or demonstrating, the noun. So this word for "warm" is something like "heartly," or "heartfelt." The woman's touch, her hand on my arm, was warm; it had the characteristic of demonstrating the heart. I moved to the other side of the escalator, she grinned and sipped her coffee, and I thought, "I'm sure your friends must love you."

○

The woman in the story of Mark, perhaps more frightened now than before, comes and tells the whole truth, not the partial truth, or the quick truth, but the whole truth.

What was the whole truth? It was the truth of her body and the truth of the commentary upon her body. It was the truth of whatever exclusion she put upon herself and whatever exclusions were forced, like torture, upon her. It was the truth of parasitical physicians and hoped-for healing. The solitary story of her clandestine touch is now a public story, and this single story is heard by the previously jostling crowd, and us, centuries later. The woman who was introduced without reference to any other friend or family member is now called "daughter," a term of endearment, reciprocality, and familiarity. Her healing is pronounced, but I always suspect that in many ways she'd already healed herself. She had not stopped herself from going to where it's likely she should not have gone. Jesus tells her, "Be healed of your flogging," and I wonder, again, at the choice of words.

The encounter with this woman draws much attention to touch, a significant feature in the Markan text. The first evangelist has Jesus taking people by the hand, stretching out his hand to touch and heal, encountering someone with a withered hand and touching or laying hands on many people—children at the point of death, sick people and people with socially excluding physical impairments. A crowd in the synagogue exclaims, "What deeds of power are being done by his hands!" and before laying his hands on children brought to him, Jesus takes them in his arms. In the light of this tender, sensory, and committed depiction of Jesus's compassionate physicality, it is striking that Mark's final mention of "hands" is in the context of violence. The one with deeds of power in his hands is now the victim of abusive power through other hands:

Then they laid hands on him and arrested him.

Hello to touch.

♀

For years I counted hugs.

One, Two, Three, Four.

One in Donegal with Annette.

Then Two, two years later, at a summer camp.

Then Three, unexpectedly, after a party.

When I was eighteen, I remember the count was up to thirty. I knew them all. Does the counting of hugs count as one loneliness or many? What I do know is that it was a far superior replacement for the comparison of body shapes and sizes with my contemporaries. To count the squeezings of the heart is to count certain encounters with others, and this is a thing shared, not a thing compared. It was not a race to a goal but a map of love traveled and love hoped for.

♥

Much is made of the death of Jesus's body: the hanging from a torture device under the weight of his own bones, skin, and meat until he suffocated. There are at least three reasons given by the New Testament writers about what it means and how it means and why it means it. I enjoy reading authors who posit the fourth and fifth and sixth whats, whys, and hows. What I also like is that it tells a story of a life lived and a life that went farther than mine.

In a gospel of hope, and in knowledge of the body, I choose to believe that Jesus of Nazareth, a man younger than me now, went where I have not yet gone so that when I go there, I will be both alone and in company.

Maybe I'll touch his body there. Maybe I'll find an embrace. Maybe this way of understanding body as truth and sharing will help me live now with a little more confidence, and a little more courage. Maybe it'll help me live in a more generous way—to my own self and to my own.

Hello to the generosity of the body.

Yearn

I've sung songs of spring
in the morning
and in the evening time
with flowers blooming and
bushes burning
offerings of love and
bitter learning

and I've sworn by heaven
and darker places
to find my way through
these nighttime cages
and I've come out
fighting angels
kissing demons
chasing strangers.

I yearn for home.

I sat for a golden afternoon
up on Thomas Ryan's
balcony.
I watched the
autumn sunlight
and I smelled the breeze.

Sitting down comfortably
on an old and broken rocking chair,
I closed my eyes
I felt the earth
and
breathed.

I yearn for home.

I've heard that Elves
have ships on which to sail away,
across the morning waters
to their gray havens
fair and far away
from here.

I wonder if all my longings
could shape for me
a ship of hopes
to carry me
on these seas of homeward yearning.

I yearn for home.

7

Hello to the shadow

> They heard the sound of the Lord God walking in the garden at the time of the evening breeze, and the man and his wife hid themselves from the presence of the Lord God among the trees of the garden. But the Lord God called to the man, and said to him, "Where are you?" He said, "I heard the sound of you in the garden, and I was afraid, because I was naked; and I hid myself." He said, "Who told you that you were naked? Have you eaten from the tree of which I commanded you not to eat?"

This is an old story, and it is a story that tells us inasmuch as it is a story that we tell. There is the Adam and there is the Eve. The Adam is a prototype of the story of males and the Eve is the prototype of the story of females, and in this way they are ideological archetypes. Earlier on in this story of creation, while the couple were still in the garden, the first words of the woman were to the serpent, thus establishing an old story that first blames women for evils before secondly blaming the serpent. When the man was asked by God why he had eaten a forbidden fruit, he answered that it had been the woman, and he blamed God and the woman—she was now "the woman you gave me." The woman, answering the question of God, said, "The serpent tricked me and I ate." The woman and the man were sent from the garden.

This is the story that many call "the Fall." The fall from what? The fall, I suppose, from a height toward a depth. A height of dignity to a deeper indignity. Some read the story as inflicting a bruise on the soul of all humanity, an original sin that affects us. Others read the story to believe that it infects the deepest realm of our capacity for good, corrupting all we do with a depravity from which we cannot save ourselves:

> Now the man knew his wife Eve, and she conceived and bore Cain, saying, "I have produced a man with the help of the Lord." Next she bore his brother Abel. Now Abel was a keeper of sheep, and Cain a tiller of the ground. In the course of time Cain brought to the Lord an offering of the fruit of the ground, and Abel for his part brought of the firstlings of his flock, their fat portions. And the Lord had regard for Abel and his offering, but for Cain and his offering he had no regard. So Cain was very angry, and his countenance fell. The Lord said to Cain, "Why are you angry, and why has your countenance fallen? If you do well, will you not be accepted? And if you

do not do well, sin is lurking at the door; its desire
is for you, but you must master it."

Just after the exit from the garden—a new beginning of a new beginning, if you like—the woman speaks again, and here, she says, "I
have produced a man with the help of the Lord." That her second
set of words is to acknowledge the production of a man is indicative
of the telling of a story of Woman through the story of Eve through
the story of the men who wrote the text.

Anyway, Eve and her three men share a tent and sin is "lurking" at the
door. Other translations render the word as "crouch" and, of course,
the door was less a hinged piece of wood and more of an entrance,
a flap in a tent. Sin, or wrongdoing, is crouching at the entrance to
the tent. And it is the responsibility of the firstborn of the firstborn of
God to resist that which lurks and crouches and turn to that which
is good. In this story we hear the story of women as told by men, we
hear the story of rivalry between brothers, we hear a story of inheritance because Genesis often honors the secondborn son instead of the
firstborn, and we hear a story of the strange ways of God, who prefers
blood to grain and who speaks with humanity. Cain doesn't kill an
animal but he does kill a brother.

These stories are used by many to speak about the beginning of
the bruise of sin in the world. What can these ancient texts have to
say to humanity about our capacity to inflict harm on one another?

In the Shelter

Hello to the ancient story.
Hello to spilled blood.

♀

I'd grown up reading Patrick Kavanagh, the Monaghan poet who loved and hated his land, his religion, his very being. As a teenager, I'd hated him, and resented his lamentations. "O stony grey soil of Monaghan," I chimed with disgust, thinking what a stupid poem it was. When I moved from Ireland, on something that was deeper than impulse, more like intuition, I bought a book of his collected poems:

> Having confessed he feels
> That he should go down on his knees and pray
> For forgiveness for his pride, for having
> Dared to view his soul from the outside.

When I was seven years old we were preparing to make our first confession. At that stage, Irish children made their first confession at the same time as they made their first holy communion. So, as a result, I tended to call my first confession my first holy confession. These days, it's called the sacrament of reconciliation, a demonstration that power lies in language, and that in order to keep living, we must sometimes rename that which is most important.

Anyway, I was a sickly child; I had as-yet-undiagnosed sadness and asthma, and so I missed the day when the teacher—the gentle-hearted Mr. Boland—instructed the class on the making of confession. As the time came near for our mock confession (the assistant principal, the tall Mr. McCarthy, stood in for the priest), I asked my friend in the lineup what I was supposed to say:

> You lied to your parents.
> You said a bad word
> and
> You hit your sister,
> he said to me.

He was six-and-three-quarters years old. He was evidencing already an aptitude for charm and creativity. He didn't even have a sister, but he knew I did.

This classmate of mine was young for the class. He was not yet seven. He was eighty-one months old, and he was lining up to step into a dark box to tell his sins.

So I stepped into the confessional box and told the teacher my sins. He gave me a mock penance. The talk in the class afterward was what sins different boys had confessed. From my analysis, most of us had lied to our mothers and either made a rude gesture or used a bad word. Some of us had stolen, some of us had hit our siblings. To our delighted horror, one boy said that he'd confessed, "I'm sorry I said 'shit' to my parents."

My class had, within it, some ingenious less-than-one-hundred-month-old boys.

The actual event was a basic rerun of the mock event; small boys lined up in newly washed uniforms, hair combed for once. I had a new set of vest and underpants (£1.99 in Penny's) for the occasion. There is the old joke about wearing fresh underwear in case you are hit by a bus. I can remember my first holy confession now with all the innocence and creativity it contained. Others can't. They, whether they were wearing freshly bought underpants or not, found in the confessional more sin than was ever confessed there.

It wasn't all priests. And it wasn't only priests. But it was mostly men. I heard of a teacher who, when angry at a child, took his keys and hit the child on the head until the child's face was covered in blood. I once saw a child being lifted off the ground when the teacher pinched his cheeks so tight that he was able to use that vise grip to lift him off the floor. The boy's cheeks remained red and raw and pinched for an hour. It could be a science question. How much force would a man in his midthirties need to exert through his torso, arms, and fingers in order to lift up an eight-year-old boy by the jaw? I am sure that there is a sinful kind of calculus that could be applied.

What is sin?

●

I know of a priest who, when overzealous friends of mine who were in their early twenties went to him for confession, used to laugh at them and say, "What would a twenty-year-old know of sin?" I like and dislike his words. I like them because he was an antidote to the selfishness that much zealous religion evidences, and I dislike them because it is unfortunately true that we can hurt each other grievously, even before the age of reason, whatever that is these days.

Hello to the shadow

Sin, in the words of James Alison, is an "addiction to being less than ourselves." In order, then, to make sense of sin, we need to make sense of ourselves, and in order to make sense of ourselves, we need to reckon with the powerful possibility that our selves are of value, and not just for a distant redeemed potential that exists like a taunting promise of what might-but-will-probably-never-be, but for now, for what is, for what is in the ordinary sacrament of today.

What is the worst sin? I wonder if this is a poor question. There are terrors and atrocities committed in the day and in the night. There are things seen and unseen, and to create a numbered list is to imagine that lists like this would work. How do you measure sorrow? By size or impact?

I heard, years ago, of a phone line in California—why is it always California?—that was never answered. The phone line was connected to an answering machine and the answering machine was wiped every day. It was like dial-a-priest, except the priest was never there, and what was there at the beginning of every day was an empty tape to which people could tell the truths that they wished weren't true. I don't know if this is true or anecdotal, but either way it is telling us something true about ourselves. There is a dignity in telling the way things are, especially when telling the way things are is a burden. For this we have friends and family, lovers, strangers, priests, and psychotherapists. We tell the person who cuts our hair, and we tell the person who takes our money at the bank. We acknowledge our failings to our children, our parents, our diaries, and our ceilings.

We tell the truth and we lie. We deny what we know, and we lie, even to ourselves.

What to do with all the pain that we both endure and cause? This is where so much sin-talk has much to offer but has lost ground. We must find a way to tell the violences of our own lives, and in so doing cause less harm.

"Here is the world," Frederick Buechner tells us. "Beautiful and terrible things will happen. Don't be afraid." And for this harsh truth, we have confession, we have table talk, we have the secrets we tell aloud and the secrets we keep. We have the sacrament of encounter, sometimes with our own private selves, sometimes with another, always—we hope—in the sight and hearing of God.

♀

The ninth chapter of the Gospel of John has a question as old as the world. The disciples have seen a man who has been blind since his birth and they wish to know the cause of his blindness. They ask whether it was his fault or the fault of his parents. In a certain sense, the disciples bring us back to the questions of the Eden story, questions of causality, blame, and punishment.

Mu, Jesus might have answered, if Jesus were Japanese. Unask the question, and ask a different one.

Who told you that you were naked, the God asked in the garden, and the Adam said, "The woman you gave me gave me something to eat." The economics of blame seem to be indigenous to us. I didn't start the fire, I just blew on it. I wonder if this is the original sin, the capacity to blame, to avoid responsibility, to throw another into the fire so that we don't burn. But then we burn with shame and the fire just gets bigger.

In the story from the Gospel of John, the question of the disciples may seem like an antiquated one, but it does not take long to unearth the modern equivalent. Those who live with HIV regularly encounter that question. "Who is to blame?" is the unasked—or sometimes asked—question. You? Was it sex? Was it drugs? Or—and I hate the premise of this question—were you "innocent"? People who have been raped have been subjected to questions about their culpability in their aggressors' incapacity to control themselves.

I find Jesus's answer to the question about the man born blind to be dated. He says that the man's blindness was the fault of neither his parents nor himself. He's blind, he says, so that God's work might be revealed in him, and then Jesus goes on to cure the man born blind. I suppose I don't mind the first part; it's the idea that the cure of blindness is the demonstration of God's glory that is problematic, and has deepened the suffering of many who'd enjoy demonstrating the glory of God as they are, not as they might be. I do not mean to minimize the experience of any who tell stories of their cures. But those stories are always the exception. I was at a retreat last year and a woman told a story of how, when her son had been ill, she had gathered groups of friends and parishioners to pray for him. He was seriously ill, but she credited prayer and medical attention for his recovery. She wished to stand up at her church meeting on the Sunday after her son's release from the hospital, and she did stand up to make an announcement. But from where she was standing she saw the face of a woman whose son had received the same amount of prayer but who had still died. She was about to attribute her son's healing to the faith of the congregation, but in a small moment, she wondered what that would say to the woman whose son had died.

♀

English does not have a word for a parent who has lost a child. It is as if the language is saying that there are some things for which there are no words. Once, at a poetry workshop I ran, a woman wrote a poem to her dead daughter:

> Since you have died,
> there has been a
>
> in our lives.

She made the namelessness of her life speak, and in using the space for which there are no words, she made it hers. Was this to the glory of God? I would understand anybody who would respond to this cruel idea with harsh words. In this way, we can see the involvement of God in our sin. Cain was a man of the soil and he brought an offering from the ground to God, but God had no regard. Eve ate from the tree but the tree was planted by someone. Such transgressions, if they can be called transgressions, are surely part of the complication of having a God. "I participated in what you put in front of me," we complain, we blame, but if anyone is worthy and capable of absorbing our blame, then it is God.

♀

Spike Milligan, the Irish passport–holding cocreator of *The Goon Show*, died in 2002, and on his grave is written *"Dúirt mé leat go raibh mé breoite"*—"I told you I was sick." He is known more as a comedian than a poet, but he was a fine poet. His poem "Me" is published in *Small Dreams of a Scorpion* and was written in Bethlehem Hospital in Highgate, during one of the many periods when his mental health was suffering and for which he was hospitalized, sometimes at his own request.

> When I die. If He says my sins are myriad
> I will ask why He made me so imperfect
> And he will say "My chisels were blunt."
> I will say *"Then why did you make so
> Many of me."*

So what is this? This is what so many of us know, the cruelty of jest, the seeming arbitrariness of our own lives, and it feels insulting to be blamed for something that is at the core of our being. Theology proposes that original sin is a wound, but not a wound implying personal guilt, just a wound that wounds the souls of all who are born. This story then seems to add injustice but no satisfactory explanation. Spike Milligan brings us back too to the garden, to the very circumstances that are blamed for humanity's flaws—Eve eating a fruit and passing it on to Adam. "Why did you do this?" Sir Spike asks God. God, in the poem, is the source of all this, and it is God who bears the brunt of blame.

If anyone can cope with our blame, it must be God.

♀

So even if we blame God, what do we do with sin, this life in a broken world? How do we respond with responsibility when responsibility itself isn't enough to overcome the complication of being human or to hurdle the devastating ways we hurt each other, even when we wish to love each other, never mind when we wish harm?

Hello to the difficulty of loving.

♀

For so much of my life, I have had what I now realize is a pathological relationship to the idea of sin. It is tied less to the concept of doing wrong and more to the anxiety of *being* wrong.

I'm not sure where I contracted such severe pathology, but I did. When I was eighteen, I was a naive, curly-haired eejit with bad clothes, six pairs of underpants, more zeal for the Lord than was good for me, not an ounce of common sense, and a pathological predilection for thinking everything was my fault or, even worse, for thinking I was a fault.

Hello to blame.

Hello to the shadow

I was working with a church group that did work in schools and parishes. In the church group, we were all dirt-poor. So anything that was going for free was a good bargain. One of the priests had heard about some free radiators—so he piled myself and a few other lads into a car to go and get the free radiators. We got talking to the couple who were getting rid of their heaters and they happened to be Swiss-French. I was delighted to practice my French—so I said to them that it had been two years since I'd been speaking any French. That was that and we were driving back, late on a Thursday night with some halfhearted, leaking radiators from a Swiss-French couple who thought we were all fools for taking what only should have been melted down . . . and I realized, with a jolt, the awful truth. I had said to them that it had been two years—*deux ans*—since I'd spoken French. But that wasn't true. It was only one year.

I knew what I had to do. I had to phone them. I had to phone the Swiss-French couple and say Sorry. *Desolé*. You know the conversation we had last night? The one where I said to you in Cork-accented French that it had been two years since I had spoken any French? Well, I'm sorry. That wasn't true. It's only been one year. I lied. I didn't mean to. I'm sorry. *Desolé. Mea culpa. Brón orm.*

The Irish phrase for saying "Sorry" is *Brón orm*. It translates literally as "sadness on me." In Irish, one conjugates the prepositional pronouns. What this means is that the word for "on me" is different from the word for "with me" or "in me." Were I to have found the words to speak the truth as I was living it, I may well have said "*brón ionam*"—"sadness in me"—but I had neither the agency nor the permission to use such words at the time.

In the Shelter

Hello to the desire for permission to be.

I had learned this sorry-saying practice from lectures from priests and nuns and laypeople about how to respond to sin. You hunted it out. It crouched near your door; you stamped on it. "Do you exaggerate?" one teacher had asked the class once. I was an Irishman who, unbeknownst to me, would spend much of his thirties telling stories, so exaggeration is an art. "Yes," I said. "Stop it," the teacher said. "It's a sin."

The Swiss-French man had given the phone number to the priest who was driving—and I saw where he'd placed the number on the dashboard. I reached out, casually, as if curious, or lightheartedly perusing the pieces of random paper on the dashboard, and I lifted up the paper. 4 37 39 30 31. I repeated it until I got home. I decided that it was too late to call the Swiss-French couple at 11 p.m., so I thought I would wait until the morning before I kept the Lord happy.

The next morning we were out again, talking to the youth of Ireland, about the Lord, and how good he is, and how he makes us all happy . . . and I made my excuses. I went to the staff room. I fished out the number from my pocket where I'd written it the night before. 4 37 39 30 31 . . . and I dialed it. It rang. It rang, and it answered. It was some company. It must have been the Swiss-French man's work number. I said, "I . . . my name is Pádraig and I want to speak with a Swiss-French man to clarify something I said to him last night when myself and some others went to pick up some radiators that he'd advertised he was giving away for free."

"What are you on about?" said the man.

"Never mind," I said. "Sorry."

Later on that night, I spoke to my colleague Siobhán. Siobhán was a nurse by training, a farming woman with five brothers. She was highly skeptical about moralism and probably the most normal, the most human, and by consequence, the most sincerely honest about religion of all of us in the group.

"Siobhán," I said, "I've got to apologize to the man we got the free radiators from, because when I was speaking in French to him last night, I said it was two years since I had spoken French and not one year. I realize that I have sinned and I need to make it right."

Siobhán, who was used to my pathological scruples, looked at me with pure incredulity. "Jesus, Mary, and Joseph," she said, "are you trying to convince him you're part of a cult?"

Hello to the truth.

I had joined the church group mostly because I hadn't been successful in getting into the college course I'd chosen. I'd always liked people so I thought I might enjoy medicine, but my results from my final exams weren't good enough. So I heard of this church group and a week after the disappointment I filled in the application form to join. The application form was twenty pages long, and it was reasonably unsurprising. It asked questions about my faith, my family, my interests, my capacity to live with people from other Christian denominations, my health, and whether I'd ever been involved in occultism, drug addiction, alcoholism, or homosexuality.

They provided four neat boxes, one for each affliction. I was to tick a box, if relevant, and use the three lines following for an explanation.

Ticking the box didn't mean exclusion, they said.

Ticking the box didn't mean exclusion in their mind, I say, but it meant everything to me.

I closed the damned application form
and put it back in its envelope.

□ □ □ □

Hello to the awful boxes.

□ □ □ □

Hello to sin crouching at the entrance.

□ □ □ □

I have always loved words. I have always loved the sound of them, the feel of them on the tongue, the play of accents, the rearrangement of letters for remaking meaning in tired syntax.

But after I first saw those damned boxes on the application form, I was wordless. I had asked one of the youth leaders to listen to me; we were outside and I was wordless, gulping air like I was drowning in it. It was at a camp in the middle of the middle of

Ireland, and I eventually remember saying that I had something
to tell him.

Even now, I can remember the feeling. Actually, that isn't true
enough. It isn't that I can remember it still; I can feel it still. It is like
a hand on my chest, a hand that may or may not hurt. It is a light-
ness of breathing, a shaking of the fingers. I went to a local church
leader and tried to talk, but I had no words. I just cried. And it
wasn't the kind of crying that brought tears. It was the kind of crying that made my throat raw. Racking, exhausting cries that shook
my body. I was a skinny runt then. I was shaking. I couldn't find
any words, so I said, "I have something to show you." I got out
the envelope with the application form. I opened the envelope
and removed the application form, and turned to the page with
its four little boxes. I pointed to the one about homosexuality.

"I have to tick that," I said, and then it
was his turn to lose his words.

☐ ☐ ☐ ☑

The next day, my voice was hoarse.

☑

So no wonder I was obsessed with being wrong, with having sin,
sorrow, and sadnzess not just on me but in me.

That night, right after I'd told a youth leader that I had to tick
that box, he sat in silence, and I sat in the awful wake of words
I'd never spoken aloud to anybody else. I had spoken them aloud

once before, to myself. We lived a mile from a village in Cork, and I waited until everybody had gone from the house. Nobody could have heard me. "I am a, I am a, I am a, I am a, I am a homosexual," I said to whoever I was hoping wasn't listening. I was trying to listen, but I could barely speak.

◉

Hello to the things we thought we'd never say.

◉

So here I was, with an application form in front of me and an abominable box waiting to be ticked. The man, who was kind but bewildered, told me a story.

He said, "A few years ago, I was at a prayer meeting, and at the prayer meeting, there was someone with the gift of healing. While the prayer meeting was going on, they stood up and said, 'There's someone here with a cyst, and if they come forward now, they are going to get healed.' I knew it was me, but I was embarrassed because I had a cyst, but the cyst was on my left testicle. I didn't want to talk about my testicles at a prayer meeting. So I stayed quiet. The healer, though, was insistent. 'There's somebody here with a cyst,' they repeated, and then when nobody came forward continued, 'The person with the cyst will be healed from their cyst if they could come forward.'"

I felt like my throat was bleeding from the crying, but the man's story was having a good effect on me. Not because I was thinking about his testicles, but because even in my miserable state I was wondering, "Of all the stories to tell, what the hell is he talking about his balls for?"

◉

Anyway, I ticked the box, and I applied and I was accepted. For a few years, I lived and worked with the church group in a joyful tumble of community and faith and prayer and work. For the most part, it was wonderful. Even three attempts to exorcise the demon of homosexuality were not enough to reduce the joy of community or, fortunately, undo what was deepest in me. One night, I remember, I got up in the dark hours and crept to where I knew the applications were stored. I opened the files and found my own. I turned to the pages with the four little boxes and looked. I had crawled inside the sinful box that both prescribed my life and described it as sin. When—years later—I began to tell more of my friends that I was gay, they were mostly kind. Those days, that's all I was hoping for— kindness. But some of them were better than kind. Some of them believed that those damned boxes indicated a wrong question. I had crawled into that little box and, cramped, decorated its walls with what I could. It was a horrible box, but in it I learned a lot.

Hello to the inside of a sinful box I should never have climbed into.

And the exorcisms were mild, I suppose. Somebody told somebody who told somebody else that the frightened boy in the corner had ticked the awful box so somebody thought that somebody was infected with the devil. And so loud prayers and words of power were used to exorcise something that wasn't wrong in the first place. I was told that *humiliation* came from the same root word as *humble,* so therefore the lesson was to eat humiliation pie because it's probably good for you. Even etymology can be diabolical sometimes.

Hello to believing that there's a world outside the box.

♀

So sin is something that we can do to ourselves and others, and sin is something that is done to us, often—and it is both sad and true to say this—by those who are proposing the antidote to sin. "Believe on the Lord Jesus Christ," they sin in the ears of those who are already burdened, "and you shall be saved."

So do we say goodbye to sin?

Goodbye and get out. Fare thee unwell. Good luck and good riddance.

And what would we be left with then?

Sin can be two things—an explanation for what happened at the start of the world, the original thing that bruised us. But it can also be a tired word to describe our capacity to bruise and kill one another. That second concept of sin—or whatever we call it—is inseparable from us. No human rights legislation, no legal framework, no moral code, no creation narrative, and no sacred text is enough to separate us from the capacity we bear in ourselves to love and hate each other. We do it so comprehensively, turning toward and turning from each other from second to second and breath to breath. But if we simply call it the other face of love, then we are removing agency, transformation, and depravity from our story, and we know that we strive for agency, celebrate transformation, and practice depravity with evidenced commitment.

What is a narrative of sin that is both prescriptive and transformative? How do we understand ourselves gently while weighing up the consequences of our actions? What is a practice adequate enough to encompass both our potential for good and our predilection for greed? Sin has two rebellious daughters, we might say. Language and Hope. Language to confess the awful truth and hope that we might move, however slowly, toward change.

I know that it would be appropriate, when discussing the Gospels, to highlight the death on the cross. But that's too easy. While the torture and death of Jesus of Nazareth was anything but easy, the formulaic "you've been saved from your sins by the death of Jesus" has been said too often, too easily, and with too little meaning. I'm thinking of the eleven-year-old girl in the De La Salle Pastoral Centre who, when she heard a version of the atonement that implied that God killed his Son and therefore we should be happy, said that she wasn't happy, or entertained. She now worried that her daddy was going to kill her.

○

Whatever Jesus of Nazareth's death means, it doesn't mean something that can be written on a fridge magnet. When I was studying theology, I had to write an essay. It was an essay that changed me because it asked whether Christians believe that we are saved by the birth of Jesus of Nazareth, by the death of Jesus of Nazareth, or by his resurrection or ascension. It was an essay to examine how well we could argue an emphasis, rather than create a supremacy of these factors within Christian theology, and I loved it. I chose the incarnation because it struck me then, and it strikes me now, that life needs to be lived, with all its complications, and that we need an avenue to incorporate hope into our lives, not just our afterlives.

The story of the incarnation of Jesus of Nazareth into the lives of ordinary people is not just a story of taking individual sins on like a heavy sack over his holy shoulder but a story of living in the midst of a society that holds hope with corruption, a society where you can be condemned for doing something good, a society that punishes those who are already punished and a society with a pathological relationship to our own capacity for good. If we are to tell the story of sin, we must tell the story of the sin we live in, not just the sins we commit. There is no satisfactory answer to the story of Adam and Eve and their two troubled sons. There would, however, be an interesting story about what it was like to leave the garden and what the sons understood their lives should be. There would be power in hearing that story told by those who are named in it.

◆

"Hope is the thing with feathers," Emily Dickinson wrote.

Recently a friend of mine was talking about visiting a relative in prison. "What do I do?" my friend said. "I want to help him hope, but I don't want him to break his heart hoping for things that'll never come true."

Hello to the shadow

The conversation got me wondering—what is the purpose of hope?

I understand that hope can break you. To hope for something that might never come true may be a difficult thing.

I was taught a class on the Prophets by a Jewish scholar and during the class, under her guidance, my imagination was captured by some words from Isaiah. I knew the verses, because my parents' prayer group used to sing a jousty song set to its lyrics:

You shall go out with joy, the song said.
And be led forth with peace.
The mountains and the hills will break forth before you, the song said.
There'll be shouts of joy
and all the trees of the field will clap their hands, the song said.

It's such an uplifting rousing chorus of independence, festival, vindication, and celebration.

It's debated when the prophet wrote these words.

One suggestion is that the prophet wrote these words while the people were in exile in Babylon. They'd been marched there from their beloved city, Jerusalem. They were in exile now, learning a different language, under the control of a foreign king in a cruel repetition of previous slavery. And in the hope of return, their prophet wrote this song. It's an imagination of return, a gladness so great even the mountains, the hills, and the trees would break forth with joy. It didn't happen. What did happen was that Cyrus, a Persian king, conquered Babylon, and the Jewish people were sent

191

back to their own city, but not with shouts of joy, just with a different power over them.

So was their song of joy a waste? Adam Phillips says that hope is only ever disproven in retrospect, so to dash hope in the moment of hoping is to have allowed a catastrophe that hasn't yet happened to already have an effect. So, no, hope is not a waste. Hope is a song sung when everything else says you shouldn't be singing. Hope is joy. Hope is a testimony that says "even if it doesn't come true, I will live like it might." Hope is what helps us survive. Hope is little light.

> Hope is the thing with feathers
> That perches in the soul,
> And sings the tune without the words,
> And never stops at all,
>
> And sweetest in the Gale is heard;
> And sore must be the storm
> That could abash the little bird
> That kept so many warm.

Hello to hope.

Hello to the shadow

The poet Paul Durcan gives us wisdom too and, before the sacrament of confession was referred to as the sacrament of reconciliation, was already mining deeper than the word would imply. In his poem "10.30 a.m. Mass, 16 June 1985," he describes the priest who said the mass. Because it was Father's Day, the priest told a story about his own father as part of the homily. The priest tells the congregation about how his father only liked one thing more than a pint of Guinness: two pints of Guinness. But the priest's proud father had given up drink as a way of giving thanks for his son's vocation to the priesthood. The priest described his dad's death:

> He died from cancer
> A few weeks before I was ordained a priest.
> I'd like to go to Confession—he said to me:
> OK—I'll go and get a priest—I said to him:
> No—don't do that—I'd prefer to talk to *you*.
> Dying, he confessed to me the story of his life.

If we are to tell a story of sin, and our experience shows us that we will always be missing the mark of our best selves, then we must tell this story within the context of the confession of the story of our lives. This is our truest dignity, to be alive, and to have a story to tell. This is the richness of becoming more and more fully our own selves.

In Durcan's poem, the priest whose father had confessed the story of his life to him was a generous man, a man who knew and loved his life and lived generously with it. He had things to confess—surely he too had hurt people—but what he confessed was not only his sin but also his truth.

Hello to the truth that we confess in our stories.

Hello to us.

Collect

God of watching,
whose gaze I doubt and rally against both,
but in which I take refuge, despite my limited vision.
Shelter me today,
against the flitting nature of my own focus,
and help me find a calm kind of standing.
And when I falter, which is likely,
give me the courage and the kindness to begin again
    with hope and coping.
For you are the one whose watchfulness is steady.
Amen.

God of silence,
who watches our growth and our decay,
who watches tsunamis and summer holidays,
who cares for the widow, the orphan,
the banker, the terrorist, the student,
the politician, the poet, the freedom fighter.
We pray to be nurtured in our own silences.
We pray that we might find in those silences
truth, compassion, fatigue and hearing.
Because you, you, you see all, and are often silent.
And we need to hope that you are not inattentive to our
needs.
Amen.

God of darkness

You must be the god of darkness

because if you are not, whom else can we turn to?

Turn to us now.

Turn to us.

Turn your face to us.

Because it is dark here.

And we are in need. We are people in need.

We can barely remember our own truth, and if you too have forgotten,

then we are without a hope of a map.

Turn to us now.

Turn to us.

Turn your face to us.

Because you turned toward us in the body of incarnation.

You turned toward us.

Amen.

8

Hello to change

My youngest brother—an engineer—tells of the joys of disproving a hypothesis. To discover that you are wrong, he says, and to discover the avenue to proving that you are wrong when you—and others—may previously have thought you were correct, is one of the aims of science. For many, the possibility of being wrong is a threat to the foundations of thought, morality, or empire. And without a doubt, those who advocate scientific thought are as prone as other schools of thought to being superior. But written into the heart of science is the embrace of the gift of being wrong.

For a long time the number 147,573,952,589,676,412,927 had been considered a prime number. Prime numbers are unusual because there is no known way to discover what sequence prime numbers have. Édouard Anatole Lucas was a French mathematician who had found a way to prove that 147,573,952,589,676,412,927 must have had factors, but he hadn't been able to prove what those factors were. That job was left to Frank Nelson Cole who, in 1903, made a presentation to the American Mathematical Society that demonstrated his love of theatricality, the joy of disproving a hypothesis, and the painstaking years he'd taken to do so. He arrived to give a lecture. The lecture, in its entirety, was without words. He wrote 147,573,952,589,676,412,927 on a board with chalk. So far, so good; the number had, among mathematicians, a certain amount of notoriety, as numbers go. To the side of this number he wrote two other numbers: 193,707,721 and 761,838,257,287. He then proceeded to multiply these two numbers, and he did this by hand. The answer to the multiplication of 193,707,721 by 761,838,257,287 is 147,573,952,589,676,412,927. Frank Nelson Cole finished his sums and sat back down, not having uttered a word during his lecture. He received a standing ovation. He had spent years working on this, and not just his professional time. He had allowed himself to be haunted by this desire to change the minds of many.

All of this goes to show that there is a capacity of human existence found in proving yourself—and sometimes others—wrong or right. His discovery meant that he, and others, had been wrong when they thought they were right. They needed to change their minds, and he'd dedicated years to that endeavor.

♀

Hello to changing our minds.

♀

The Gospel of Mark includes strong language at the beginning.

> John the Baptizer appeared in the wilderness, proclaim-
> ing a baptism of repentance for the forgiveness of sins.

Hello to change

The word *repentance* has become known as strong language. It has been used as a bludgeon or a burden on so many for so long that its original richness may be in danger of being lost—if it hasn't been already. The Greek word translated into English as "repentance" is *metanoia*. The prefix *meta* means "beyond," hence *metaphysics* being the study of—or speculation about—what is beyond the natural. The word *noia* means "thought" or "mind." Together, however, *metanoia* means to change your thoughts, to change your mind, to turn in a new direction, to reverse a direction and go a different way.

Hello to new directions.

Technically, then, this should mean that the Christian faith is a faith that is adapted to change, a faith that is not undone by realizing that its precepts or propositions are incorrect. It should mean that the joy of repentance is evidenced—over and over and over and over—by those who practice the Christian faith. It should mean that Christianity would be known as the faith that regularly announces that it has, hitherto, been wrong and is neither frightened nor undone by discovering error or misdirection.

Here's another bit of Greek. A Greek word for "sin" is *hamartia*, which means "to miss the mark." So when we discover that we are missing the mark, we reorient our direction.

🎯

When Gandhi arrived in Britain, it's reputed that he was asked by an English politician, "So, Mr. Gandhi, what are your impressions of Christian society?" "It's a nice idea," Gandhi reportedly replied. It was a good answer, because it is a nice idea. However, it's also an idea—but not a nice one—that empire has ever been an indicator of Christian morality.

♀

The call to repentance comes from unusual sources. Once, I was getting a boat from Melbourne to Tasmania, and while I love boats, I need to feel the fresh air, so I was hanging on to the railings. I got speaking to a man, and as is the wont of conversations, the talk turned to religion. I was telling him of my love for words and how I wish that the word *repentance* was more richly appreciated. I asked him what he thought of that. "I'm an atheist," he said, "but I think you need to repent," and then he repeated to me some flippant comment I'd made to him early in our conversation that indicated prejudice. He was right. He was putting me to the test and I had come up short. I needed to repent. "Handsome is as handsome does," wrote Jane Austen in a letter to her beloved sister, Cassandra. She conjectured that Mr. Digwood, who had used them basely, was therefore a "very ill-looking man." I suppose the sentiment can be echoed here. Repenting is as repentance does, and they that talk but do not do are therefore unrepentant.

♀

Three of the four Gospel accounts indicate that Jesus was tempted in the desert by the devil. Mark's account is a short sentence, but Matthew's and Luke's are more detailed. Matthew's and Luke's versions contain much the same content, but told in a notably different order.

Hello to change

In Matthew's version, in the fourth chapter, Jesus is led by the spirit into the desert—the wilderness, a lonely place—to be tempted by the devil. When I was nine, I asked for a Bible for a Christmas present, and my parents bought me a splendid volume, written accessibly for zealous nine-year-olds, complete with pictures. It was Christmas Day 1984 and I leafed through the pages until I found a picture of the devil. Here he was, in the desert with Jesus, and he was sky blue. He had a tail, and eyes of fire. It was magnificent and frightening all at once, just like religion, just like life.

The devil is called two things in Matthew's version—the *diabolos*, meaning "slanderer" or "devil," and *peirazō*, "the one who tempts." But the word for "tempter" comes from a word exploring proof, so I prefer the second word because it's a moveable title, as we all know that anyone can put anyone to the proof. The tempter, the proof-tester, was putting a hypothesis to the test, and his hypothesis is curiouser than it seems.

The tempter says to Jesus,

> If you're the Son of God, turn these stones into bread.
> If you're the Son of God, throw yourself from the
>   temple.
> I'll give you all the kingdoms of the world if you
>   worship me.

Luke's version has the second and third temptations in a different order, but Luke's Gospel is all about the long slow journey to Jerusalem, so it's no wonder that the final temptation in Luke is on the temple in Jerusalem.

In the early 1990s, BBC Radio 4 broadcast a play about the temptations of Jesus in the desert. It was magnificent and featured the three traditional temptations followed by other, less known ones. Jesus was tempted by a blackberry-flavored wine gum but manfully resisted. He finally caved in when offered the opportunity to crack the foil on the top of a coffee jar with the back of a teaspoon. It produces such a pleasing *thock* sound.

There's a subtlety in these scriptural versions of proof tests, however. The word *if* can be understood to imply "if you are who you say you are, then you'll be able to turn the stones to bread," with the direct correlation of "if you don't, then maybe you're not who you say you are." But the Greek word *ei*, translated here as "if," is akin to "since" or "that," so the temptations may be better read as saying, "Because you are you, why don't you do this?" It wasn't a challenge to Jesus's identity, it was a challenge to his power. It was a temptation that said,

> You are capable of many things. So do what you like.
> Use your power in this way.

Suddenly, it isn't a sky-blue devil with cloven feet and a fork in a desert east of the Mediterranean. It is every day. It is the complication of every moment. Because I am capable of this feat of power, or this feat of management, or this feat of ordering, do it. Do it. Do it. It doesn't matter. You're capable of it.

We see the linkage between temptation and power and capacity and inconsideration.

Hello to temptation. It's rarely as obvious as we'd like.

In the story of Jesus in the desert, we hear—albeit obliqued by the drama of the *diabolos*—a story of humanity. The first temptation that Jesus faced was to use power to serve his own good and, in addition, to turn back on what he had committed to do. He was in the desert using hunger so he could face himself, and here he was tempted to cease the very project he'd undertaken. You're capable of so much more than this, he was hearing; take a shortcut. Take an easy way out. You've started well; why not finish early?

It is a temptation that many of us know well.

The second temptation of Matthew—the third of Luke—is to throw himself from the temple. There are religious ways of reading this, but lately I've been struck by the stark truth of this. Throw yourself from a height. Kill yourself. End it all. Life can be overwhelming, and potential is sometimes as fearsome a thing as limitation. In the face of the truth of who he was, we have a story of Jesus of Nazareth that considers the possibility of ending.

And the last temptation—to worship at the feet of misguided power—is to mistake an end goal of meaning for a meaningless trip of power. At various points in our lives, we each face these proof tests, and the question isn't whether we are or are not gods; the question is whether we are going to use our capacity to shortcut, to destroy or violate the art of being human.

Hello to the temptation to take the easy way out.

Hello to the temptation to self-destruct.

Hello to the temptation to worship what will serve you.

In the Shelter

My friend Rory is a man of generosity and insight. Once, while I was still working in a religious environment where it was difficult to be gay, we were talking. I was describing—like a broken record, I imagine—the conundrum that I was facing about whether I'd remain working for this group that I loved or whether it was time to leave.

Rory speaks in a considered way. He said, "What strikes me about you is that, in all of the decisions about your life, you're committed to . . ."

I prepared myself for a display of modesty.

". . . making things as difficult for yourself as possible." I was not prepared for this.

Hello to the shock of the truth.

We were driving at the time—and I could bring anybody to the turn in the road where I remember those words were said—and driving allows for silence. I was silent a long time while I viewed my decisions through this lens. It wasn't the only lens through which to view my decisions, but it was a damned powerful one. In the midst of my having good reasons to resent and require the religious life I had chosen, Rory's words were inviting me to a new kind of growing up, a new kind of responsibility. It is no surprise that a year later, again while staying with Rory, I found myself able to make decisions that had taken a decade of consideration. His welcome is always warm. So is his warning.

It seems that much of what religion calls repentance is another way of saying "take responsibility." It's not always easy; it sometimes requires us to change and it takes sharp words.

Hello to change

Hello to responsibility.

If religion is going to help us, if our spirituality is going to mean something, then it must help us in our growing up. It must not speed this unnecessarily, but if it does the opposite, if it slows it unnecessarily, or even permanently, then it is a fearsome thing indeed.

Hello to growing up.

What happens to some people, I have wondered, when they cross the door into the place of worship? People who demonstrate savvy and insight in their homes, their neighborhoods, their places of work, and their places of relationship seem sometimes to be powerless to use that same agency when it comes to navigating the ways of spirituality. "My priest told me that all gay people are liars," I heard once from a person who held much responsibility at their workplace. "My minister said that the Bible said it's wrong," one man said when justifying why he had told a woman to shut up when she spoke in a prayer meeting. He worked in a company that was led by a woman, and he was a vocal supporter of her leadership and skills. Mind you, I've heard similar things from other avenues. "All religious people are deranged," I've heard from those who trust their own readings of religious people and not religious people's reading of religious people.

Repentance acts as an antidote to childishness. It asks for action, and is not satisfied with sorrow. You can be sorry all you like, but change is the fruit of responsibility. Fine words butter no parsnips, we hear, and while Irish tells us that *bíonn gach tosach lag*—every beginning is weak—the art is to begin, not just to lament.

♦

Once, years ago when I lived overseas, somebody heard that I held an occasional meal in my house for people who were lesbian, gay, or bisexual. We were all people who were haunted and loved by God, and all had found the welcome of the church to be more airy than substantial, having endured plenty of harsh words by people who justified the effects of those same words by stating idealized intentions. So, from time to time, a gang of us would eat a meal, would discuss our faith, and would find a bit of community around a table.

I got a phone call. "The priest has heard that lots of gay people are hurt by the church and is keen to be seen to respond. He's heard that you hold a meeting in your house for gay people," the voice said, "and the priest would like to come."

The story could be understood in a few ways, but it is true that the words used were that the priest was keen to be seen to respond. I phoned the priest and I asked the priest for a coffee. He came, and he brought a bottle of wine. We're still friends. But I needed to tell him that his presence was less welcome at the table of the excluded than he'd hope, because some people feared his firing power, and others feared his preaching tongue, and others feared his descriptions of our intrinsic moral disorders from the pulpit. He wasn't gay, he told me, and I believe him. So what we need to see, I told him, was less his kind words around the privacy of a table and more his public words in the halls of the powerful. Show us your change, please, I asked. Show us your change.

I wanted to say hello to his public words of repentance for bothering us with his words of power.

◊

I tried to repent from being gay. It wasn't pretty and it didn't work. Having been the recipient of the message of heteronormativity since the age of early reason, I tried everything I could manage to persuade my inner life toward the acceptable. Once I discovered prayer, I tried that too. After the successless exorcisms of my later teens, when I found out that even my naivete couldn't withstand the insult of such diabolical projections, I tried counseling and prayer ministry. Obviously, those didn't work either, and they convinced me of the vacuousness of the theory base of such interventions. This all took a while, and all the while repentance was calling. In order to grow up, I didn't need to leave God and turn toward my base sexuality. I needed to turn toward God and accept the truth. The complicated call for me was to repent from my frightened life and to turn toward the gospel.

The cartoon dog Snoopy has wisdom, for those of us who listen. Snoopy the sage is sitting on top of his doghouse and typing on his typewriter. Charlie Brown comes along and says, "I hear you're writing a book of theology. I hope you have a good title." Snoopy looks up, in a superior fashion, and indicates that he has the perfect title. He resumes typing and the title of his theological oeuvre appears in typeface in the sky. "Have you ever considered that you might be wrong?" is the perfect title to his book. It's a fine question. I remember quoting it in an essay on ecclesiology and I got the equivalent of an academic chortle back from my supervisor. It is evidence of religious integrity to be fluent in living well with the questions underneath our hope. "Let us cling to you," we say to our Jesus, and he answers, "Have you ever considered that you might be wrong?" He says, "No, do not cling to me." He says, "Live well" and "Change" and "Learn." He asks, "What are you doing with your power?" and he answers, "Do not miss the mark again." He praises those who act and criticizes those who focus only on their words. He tells stories that do not end and ends stories that don't start.

Hello to the gift of being wrong.

Hello to the need for change.

♀

In Luke's telling of the temptation in the desert, Jesus returns from the desert and announces his public work. His reputation becomes widely known and then Luke describes a particular day in a particular location. Jesus came to the place where he had been brought up, and when the time came for the text to be read, he stood up to read. The scroll of text given to him was that of the prophet Isaiah, so he opened it to a particular place and read about how the anointing had come to him to speak good news to the poor, release to the captives, sight to the blind, and freedom for the oppressed, and to announce the year of the favor of God.

Hello to change

This, then, was the response to the testing of his power. The tempter had said to him, *Because* you are who you say you are, use your power for self-gain, let your power destruct you, or use your power for increasing power. The response in the moment was to return to the Jewish faith that he loved and by which he lived. Then his response in public was to use his words, his charisma, his invitation to speak words of life and goodness toward those whose circumstances meant that they were alienated, chained up, judged, overlooked, and disenfranchised.

This, in the proofing of the Gospels, is the test of inner virtue. Not the declaration of the purity of your virtue, but the inhabiting of the outworking of that virtue toward those who have been dispossessed, even of the agency by which they themselves will rise and speak.

The text goes on to tell of how initially the response to Jesus was positive, and people wondered how the son of Joseph could speak such things. But it seems that Jesus was made uncomfortable with such praise, because he then proceeded to irritate—or perhaps you could argue that he insulted—the people. He spoke to the texts that all Jewish people hold dear and spoke of Elijah who, when he was in need, went to the home of a foreign widow and his presence brought blessing. Then Jesus spoke of Elijah's successor, Elisha, who, while there were many people suffering at the time, cured a Syrian, not a local. He was upsetting the status quo, he was noting that entitlement does not stand alone, and that responsibility is as responsibility takes, and that neither sentiment nor intention is enough.

The people sought to silence him. No wonder. He was saying unpopular things. We've been silencing him ever since.

In the Shelter

When I was a teenager, I was struck with the particular desire to work as a medical missionary. I'd met an Irish doctor who'd worked in Uganda and I found her to be an exceptional human being, so therefore I imagined myself in a similar vein. While I always knew that the family scientific genes hadn't grown in me, I thought that hard work would be enough, so I applied for medical school. I didn't get in, however. I did join a missionary society, though, and did pastoral and parish work for over a decade. But I still relished the fantasy of living in a country in Africa. It was the content of my regular prayers that I be sent somewhere foreign by the God who'd give me skills to share and capacity to partner once I was there. It wasn't necessarily an awful intention; I'd learned from enough people that service overseas is service *with*, not service *to* or service *for*. I was entranced—still am, really—with the idea of living somewhere foreign and having to learn a new language.

My prayers were full of the hope of a missionary calling, and from time to time my prayers were answered.

One day—I was at home visiting my parents in Cork—I was praying and informing God, myself, and whoever else was listening that I would go anywhere. In the midst of the prayer, my imagination was caught by a solitary thought. *Will you work with the Travellers?*

I understood it to be a question that was designed to unearth me, a question to upset the stated intentions by which I was deceiving myself. The word in Irish for the Travelling Community is *an lucht siúil*, literally translating as "the walking people," referring to the traditional practice of nomadism among the Travellers. Before I knew them by the name by which they know themselves, I knew them by the derogatory names given to them by us, the settled people. The Irish Travelling Community is an ethnic grouping who've been part of Irish society for centuries. Their culture is notable for its history, language, family traditions, and nomadism—whether in principle or in practice. The Irish Traveller experience has been weighted too by decades—and probably centuries—of misunderstanding, prejudice, and stereotyping about their lifestyle, culture, and richness. I had never met a person from the Travelling Community before, and I didn't until a few years after this experience. But I noted fear. Fear of what? I'm not sure. Fear of what I didn't understand, and perhaps willfully misunderstood. I noted the fear of association, or the fear of a downplayed demonstration of the virtue I was so adept at fantasizing about. My experience in prayer was an experience of repentance. I was so entranced by my notions of service that I was removing myself from the possibility of needing to be the recipient of service rather than the demonstrator of such service. It required a change of mind, and it began in the imagination, and nurtured curiosity and, in time, bore the possibility of real change of practice in my understanding of—and relationship with—a community that was as Irish as I was.

Hello to prejudice.

♀

Since beginning to tell the truth of my sexual orientation more widely, a number of things have happened. First, I have begun to realize the taste of relief. It is always a good thing to tell the truth. I have also found myself on the outside of the halls of holiness. I was always one for the system and willing to tolerate the complications of a structure for the greater good of the products of the structure. In that way, I'd have found some energy for being part of a large religious organism, as I'm loyal to a fault. However, without wishing it, I have become a voice that speaks from the outside, and not from the inside. It's not something I've wished for.

I've found myself with questions about privilege. When I hear the question "Why do you need gay pride parades?" I wonder how others would cope with hearing four-year-olds on your street call you "queer" in an obvious echo of the table talk in their homes. I think that if there is only one day of the year when queer couples can hold hands publicly, knowing that they will not necessarily be derided for that, then there is every need for a pride parade. "Why do you need to come out?" I have been asked, followed by an "I never felt the need to announce my sexuality." I find myself wondering when this person first whispered news of a crush on a girl or a boy to a friend, a sibling, a parent. I look at their wedding ring and hear the plural prepositions used when speaking about weekend activities or holidays and think that coming out is for everyone, it's just that some of us have to face violence when we do it.

In all of this, I find myself nurtured by the gospel because the gospel teaches us to love the word "repentance." Change your mind, I hear over and over. Change your mind is directed toward the privileged and the marginalized both. Each has the capacity to define themselves against the other.

Hello to change

A man asked a question at the end of a retreat once. It was a retreat for Christian people who were uncomfortable or cautious or unsure about how to engage with lesbian, gay, bisexual, and transgender (LGBT) people. It was a two-day retreat, with shared meals, residential accommodation, shared cups of tea, risky conversation, and the possibility of human connection. The man who asked the question had introduced himself, in his own words, as a fundamentalist Christian. It struck me as strong and deliberate language to use when speaking of self. But I've got a fondness for hearing how people choose to speak about themselves, and it's not up to me to impose my words for a group, so I was moved to hear his dedication to the words he most wanted.

The retreat went as was to be expected—which is to say, it went on with carefully mediated steps where individuals take steps toward each other in tentative understanding.

At the end of the retreat, the man asked his question. "I have a question for the gay people in the room," he began. "Since we met together yesterday," he said, "how many times have my words bruised you?" Those were his exact words. He repeated them. The LGBT people in the room—there were a few of us who'd been invited to participate in this project—were silent for a while. Irish people, while I know that we have reputations for quick tempers, are nonetheless polite, especially in a situation like this, where the man's question was so disarming. The gay man next to me said, "Ah, you're grand. Don't worry." The man who called himself a fundamentalist Christian said, "No, please. I am asking a question and I want you to answer. How many times, since we met together yesterday, have my words bruised you?" A woman sitting near me started to count on her fingers. Everybody was watching her. She counted on one hand and then the other and then said, in a quiet voice, "I gave up after the first hour." It was a hard truth, and it was a truth that took courage to ask and say.

The man with the question continued with another question: "Do you mean to say that every time you come to meet people like me, you have to prepare to put up with insult?" "Yes," was the answer. The man who called himself a fundamentalist looked at us and said, "I am glad you told me this. I have learned something."

I began to reframe how I understand the word *fundamentalist*. I was moved by his unflinching capacity to hold himself to his own questioning. He was harsher with himself than any of us were, and his words to himself went deeper into himself because the integrity of his questioning was matched by the integrity of his willingness to hear and change and respond. I am not sure who was the most repentant, him or me.

Hello to repentance.

Hello to the gift of change.

♀

Mark's Gospel does not have a detailed story of the temptation in the desert. However, it does have a story of repentance.

Jesus has gone from the territory of Galilee and is in a house in Tyre, in the south of Lebanon. It seems he is in need of a break, or a rest, or at least is desiring the possibility of noninterruption, so he makes his way to a house. He is interrupted.

Hello to interruption.

A woman comes to the house and says that there is a devil in her daughter. He responds to her by saying it isn't right that food meant for children should be given to little dogs.

This short text is a test for how we will read the Gospels. I have heard people say that he was calling her a little dog, and that little dogs are possibly puppies, and that puppies are cute, so he was either complimenting her or clearly joking. This is unlikely. In the culture of the time, and certainly in the location, it is neither cute nor funny to call someone a bitch.

She, however, seems to be perfectly capable of responding, and this is perhaps why the response is noted. She quips, "Oh, but sir, even the little dogs eat the little crumbs."

And there is a moment of repentance. The mind of the Son of the Sky is changed and he says, "Because of what you have said, the devil is gone from your daughter." It is easy to get lost in the detail of the devil, but the first part of the sentence is what is most interesting: "Because of what you have said." No one else in the Gospels, not a woman or a man, is honored in such a way. Because of what you have said. To be open to the possibility of repentance is a sign of the goodness of humanity. To consider oneself immune from the need for such changing of tune, of mind, of direction or idea is to alienate oneself from the argument of being human.

Hello to the gift of being wrong.

Hello to the gift of repentance.

Hello to change.

After the Confession

After the confession
he looked relieved
and also anxious to leave.

I am no one's priest
but I know that
such tellings leave

small exhaustions
in their wake.
He told me, a week later,

god, I slept soundly
that night—
I believed him.

Is confession given, taken, or
done?
Like all gods,

it's more
than
one.

9

Hello to power

When I first moved to Belfast I lived in a cul-de-sac near Clonard Monastery in West Belfast. There were a bunch of lads who lived on the street and my relationship with them usually consisted of me asking—read: telling; pleading with; shouting at; yelling at—them to leave my back garden when they hopped over the fence in the middle of the night to use my outdoor tap to fill plastic bottles with water, play games, throw stones, and get high.

One summer evening I was cycling home and the lads were having a barbecue on the street. It was a festival atmosphere: somebody had put some music on, there were cheap buns and cheaper burgers, some bottles of beer and ketchup. One of them offered me a burger and I was happy to find a way to talk with them properly. I knew that they were nice lads, and I was glad to chat with them, even over cheap burgers on a street covered in dog shit and broken glass. One of them asked me what I did. That has rarely had a straightforward answer for me, so I said, "I do a bit of work at the monastery around the corner, I do a bit of work in schools, and I study theology." To my surprise, they demonstrated notable interest in my theological studies. The lads I was talking to called some of the others around and said, "Pádraig studies theology." I was genuinely shocked. The ensuing question clarified everything.

"What do you think of *The Da Vinci Code*?" one of them asked.

It all became clear. This was the year that the film version of the book had been released, the book that speaks of secrets and sex rites at the heart of the Vatican, describes the halls of power of Opus Dei, and tells the story of the children of the children of the children of Jesus of Nazareth and Mary Magdalene. I said to the lads that I thought the book was entertaining enough as fiction, but not anything that should be used to understand religion. Then one of them said something that was entirely appropriate for usage in understanding religion.

"I think it's shite. Jesus was a Catholic—he wouldn't have married a whore."

The lads agreed and I tried to mention that Jesus was, in fact, a Jew, but the conversation had moved on to other films. I finished the burger, mostly grateful for a chance to have chatted properly with my neighbors. The relationships did indeed improve as time went by and as the lads grew up. I've never forgotten the phrase, though. It strikes me as something entirely revelatory of certain forms of religious education—not just formal religious education through academic or sacramental learning but broad religious education where religion is a tribal identifier. This was Belfast, after all; Catholicism means much more than how you understand the notion of transubstantiation or whether you pray for the souls in purgatory or not.

By saying that Jesus was a Catholic, the teenager on my street was, in a way, saying "Jesus was one of us." And the following clause built on this. By understanding Jesus as from among their own tribe, the logic was that tribes understand what their other members would—and especially wouldn't—do. He was saying, "Jesus is one of us, and because he was one of us, he wouldn't do *that*"—whatever *that* was. It played too on the mistaken readings of Mary Magdalene's characterization in the Gospels. In addition, even if she had worked in prostitution, and had Jesus been the marrying kind, I imagine that they'd have treated rules that proscribe marriage with the same charm and analysis as they did many other rules.

Hello to our idea of who we are.

The whole engagement struck me as the underbelly of religion. If religion tells me who I am, then it may also tell me who I'm not. And if religion tells me who else is part of my crowd, then it'll tell me who is not. The borders established around religion are often more ideological than phenomenological. The teenager on my street didn't say, "Jesus was a Catholic, he *didn't* marry a whore," he said "*wouldn't*"—and the conditional tense indicates some kind of litmus test. What would have happened if they had discovered that Jesus did marry a woman who'd worked in prostitution? What would have happened then? Would Jesus have suddenly been demoted to Protestantism, with the implication being that that's the kind of thing that *they* do?

◉

Hello to the borders we need.

In the Shelter

○

Jesus's anxiety—and it is a shame that our liturgical and sacramental life does not reflect more profoundly on the anxieties of the incarnation—seems to be evoked when religion is used as a tribal identifier, with the borders being guarded fiercely for fear that porous borders offer poor belonging. As I'm writing I'm struck by the fact that one of the Irish word for "border"—*teorainn*—can also translate as "limitation." When our borders of belonging are predicated more on defining ourselves based on who we are not, and virtues are presumed present on one side of the border and presumed missing on the other, then our borders speak more of hostility than of any sense of kinship.

The economy of this kind of bordermaking creates concrete categories. If you are to be one of us, then you will act in this way. If we find that you act in another way, then it isn't just that you aren't one of us *anymore*, it's that you never were one of us in the first place. This is a border marking that puts mines at the borderlands. Its clear categorization is nurtured more by ideology—our idea of who we should be—than by the infinitely more complicated truth of who we actually are and what we have done.

○

All of this Catholic and Protestant stuff can sound particularly Irish. I suppose, to be accurate, it's particularly Irish and British, because that's mostly what's going on. Is the north of Ireland British or Irish?

Hello to power

Who should be in power there? What performance of power is justifiable to defend or change the powers there now? It's been a bloody legacy here; our manifestation of the fight for belonging. Our struggling attempts here to address that do not give any template for how other parts of the world can address their sectarianism. All unhappy countries are unhappy in their own way, perhaps. But there can be some sharing, of ideas if not insights. Cecelia Clegg and Joe Liechty wrote an extraordinary book called *Moving Beyond Sectarianism* that attempts to plot landscapes of belonging in a place where belonging has turned bitter. They sketched out different levels of belonging in eleven statements that move from "we are right" to "you are demonic." In between these polarities of language, they make subtle points:

Sometimes I'll defend my right to say you're wrong because your point of view threatens my life, whereas my point of view just invites you to change your mind.

It'd be easy to have a quick answer to the belongings that bomb us.

Hello to the absence of quick answers.

Hello to our sharp words.

Belonging creates and undoes us both. If spirituality does not speak to this power, then it speaks to little.

Hello to power.

♀

I've read that the three questions that haunt many people are: Who am I? What am I doing here? and Where am I going?

They aren't bad questions. They point to existential anxieties and to the idea that there are particular answers to them. When I was more involved in charismatic Christianity, I remember noting how often the prophecies delivered responded to these questions. We are children of God, we were told, and then there was usually a lot of talk about "for such a time as this" followed by details of blazing light to nations and divine destinies. Some of those, to be truthful, were insightful. Most were well meant, I believe, and a few had disastrous consequences when people acted on them.

Hello to the desire for destiny.

The idea that religious experience will give a solid answer to these fundamental questions is problematic. Both Irish and English have equivalent phrases of distant hills being greener than the nearer ones, and direct experience of God is a distant hill, the summit of which brings fantasized clarity. However, what is important to question is not the answer but the idea of an answer. The word *idea* seems to be influenced by Platonic philosophy, where things exist in an ideal form or prototype. So the idea of an answer is the perfect answer, the answer upon which everything rests, the answer that will make everything clear. It is like the tempting fruit, the thing that will help us, like the God we worship, to know evil from good. Freudians make much of the narrative detail that the idea of such discernment came from an animal representing a phallic symbol, a symbol of power. To have the answer to the questions that frustrate our desire for certainty is a power greater than many. I can understand why the Eve in the garden sought the taste of such certainty, and from time to time, I can understand why it is the temptation that cannot be removed from us. It, like the tempting tree and like the primordial chaos, is simply always there, and to deny the power of the idea is to deny something fundamental about our existence.

Hello to the lack of a solid answer.

♀

In Middle Earth, there is an exchange. Merry, a Hobbit, has lost his fondest friend and is alone among men, wizards, and elves. He felt like he was in everybody's way, but a king offers him a place as an esquire. Merry is filled with love and pledges his service. His service is accepted and he says to the king, "As a father you shall be to me." But the king is wise and has only recently emerged from the deepest shadow of himself. He understands that time passes and time brings change, and that no function is powerful enough to fulfill our deepest desires. He answers, "For a little while."

Hello to the temporary answer.

♀

So we are haunted by these questions that evade the idea of an answer, because often when we achieve what we think is an answer, we find ourselves on a deeper level of the question.

Hello to the unanswerable questions.

Our relationship with power, and our desire to use power to subdue questions that undo us, is one of the projects of religious texts. In the face of fundamental questions and answers that haunt rather than console us, we land in a narrative of complicated people evolving through understanding, story, revelation, and failure. Their idea of God begins as one thing and changes to another. The stories of God that they tell each other deepen and build, and God moves from being God among Gods, to God above all Gods, to God of Gods, to God who needs nothing else.

Within the Christian story, this is the God who undoes God in the small hungry body of incarnation. This is God of God learning to walk on wobbly legs. This is the God who names God in the voice of a man who is faced with the complication of his own power. Will he use his words for complicity or consolation or something entirely different?

Hello to the answers that are lived by risk, not told by words.

When I did my undergraduate degree, I was thinking of the priesthood, so I decided to do a pontifical degree in theology, with the idea that at least I could get some of the training out of the way. Theology is—like most humanities—an art of words. And words have power. I encountered the wisdom of the apophatic traditions: it's easier to name what God is *not* than what God is.

Such humility was powerful, but some powers are threatened by humility.

May the mighty be cast from their thrones. Hello to the Mother of God.

When Moses encounters the Fire that is burning—but not consuming—a bush in the desert, he asks the Fire its name, and the Fire gives an ungraspable name because to give something a name is to give something power. By giving another group a new name we land on a power over them, especially, especially, especially if we can get the group to replace their name for them with our name for them.

On the Liechty and Clegg scale of sectarianism, there are three elements that deal with the power of naming. The first of these three indicates that "you are a less adequate version of what we are." The next says, "You are not what you say you are." And the final in this sequence declares, "We are in fact what you say you are."

◉

Hello to power.

◉

Hello to disinheritance.

◉

Hello to the God who gave up God's name.

In the Shelter

I've taught some poetry classes in schools around Belfast for a few years, and an enjoyable exercise is to take William Carlos Williams's poem "This Is Just to Say" and either rewrite or extend it. The poem, seemingly addressed to the poet's wife, says,

> I have eaten
> the plums
> that were in
> the icebox
>
> and which
> you were probably
> saving
> for breakfast
>
> Forgive me
> they were delicious
> so sweet
> and so cold

There are countless examples of school groups or adult groups who have rewritten the poem. The exercise can tap—playfully—into our deepest revenge impulses and deceives us into an enjoyable game of articulating hollow and revealing reasons. Once, a boy wrote a letter, addressed to his teacher, saying that he'd sent all the girls away on a ship to an island where they could finally be by themselves. He was ten years old and was writing his new version of an old story—a story of young boys' derision and desire for girls. His poem implied that it would be a punishment for the girls to get what they wanted. The girls in question—the ten-year-old girls in his class—gave shouts of victory at the idea. Another student, however, landed on a different kind of power. Her poem was something akin to this:

> I have stolen
> your dog
> that I know
> you loved
>
> and have
> given him
> a new
> name
>
> He is mine
> now
> I'm not sorry
> at all

She and her friend had written revenge poems to each other and the class pealed with laughter at her magnificence. I was amazed at her poetic prowess. She had discerned, and named, something at the core of marketing, religion, and politics: power. It was as if she, in her ten-year-old body, was a mirror to the world that told us of ourselves. She said, "If you rename something you have power over it."

Hello to power, so elegantly understood.

♀

In 2013, I traveled to Uganda. I had been there once before, in 1996, and had fond memories of my short time there. In 2013, I returned as a researcher to explore support given for the then proposed Anti-Homosexuality Bill by Christians—clerics and laypeople from across Catholic, Protestant, and Orthodox divides. Homosexuality was already illegal in Uganda—since the 1950 Penal Code that punished carnal knowledge against the order of nature between two men. This was updated in 2000 to a more gender-encompassing version that also covered women. In 2009, a parliamentarian proposed that a new Anti-Homosexuality Bill should be introduced—a bill that initially proposed the death penalty for some offenses. Over the course of five years, the bill went through some amendments, many controversies, became a double-edged sword when some of its public proponents began accusing each other of being gay, and was eventually passed into law—with the death penalty replaced by life imprisonment—in early 2014. In August 2014 the bill was overturned due to a technicality—there hadn't been a sufficient quorum when the bill was passed through the lower house. It remains to be seen whether this technicality will affect the impetus evident in religious, social, and governmental circles in favor of enhanced criminalization of lesbian, gay, bisexual, and transgender people.

Much public support for such laws rests on the idea that lesbian, gay, bisexual, and transgender people are a threat to children. The association of ideas with ideas is a clever thing indeed—if I can get you to think "hypocrite" when I mention "Pharisee," I have won a powerful game. If I can get you to think "immoral" or "pedophile" or "threat to life and the family" when I mention another group, then control is in my hands, and my opponents would be right to fear me.

Hello to the power of fear.

Uganda, like so many countries worldwide, has known the invasion of colonization, with its independence only having been granted in 1962. So, much Ugandan outrage at European statements against the Anti-Homosexuality Bill was based on the understanding that erstwhile colonial powers cannot become self-appointed moral arbiters. This was felt to be especially true in matters to do with internal legislative debates in a parliament the independence of which was hard won. The bill was justified as being both an extension of natural law and protection against people who are "homosexual for mercenary reasons." It was accepted by some Ugandan civic outlets that people are "turned" gay by Western charities for financial incentive.

Hello to the long and slow effect of colonization.

Part of what is so fail-safe in this schema is that much moral objection to the Anti-Homosexuality legislation is already preempted by ideas that categorize anybody who may wish to question the law as unpatriotic, or immoral, or financially suspicious. To raise debate is to already be seen to have taken many steps too far. This hasn't stopped many brave people in raising objections; however, some have paid for their objection with their lives. Many—but not enough—people have named themselves publicly and raised challenges against the legality of the bill. A former vice president of Uganda, Dr. Speciosa Wandira Kazibwe, has also issued public statements of support for Uganda's LGBT population.

What does the gospel have to say to this? What hellos can be recommended for those most affected by this law?

Hello to fear.

Hello to other people's power.

And where is the hello to God in the midst of this? Is it appropriate to believe in the impartiality of a God in whose name abominable laws are passed against those called abominations in the text of that same God?

I traveled to Uganda to meet with church leaders and faith workers to explore their readings of Gospel texts. I had written a dissertation on "Jesus and the marginalized" and had focused particularly on how the authors of the Gospels of Luke and Mark had characterized the marginalized characters—often especially the morally marginalized characters—as not only people worthy of charity but people who were honored as displaying the very virtues claimed by the righteous. The marginalized are, in the literary projects of Mark and Luke, the teachers of those who claim their entitlement at the center of society. Given this, I was curious about whether discussions about the marginalized in the Gospels could open religious conversations with Christians who work for the public good.

Hello to the margins. They have much to teach us about power.

It was a short visit, filled with many things. It was filled with warm hospitality and shared food. It was filled with curiosity and kindness. It was filled with the assumption that the researcher—an Irishman who obscured the spelling of his name to make it ungoogleable—was a Christian "just like us," and it was filled with faith and fear, power and promise.

In seminars and interviews, I, together with generous and committed Ugandan Christians, explored the text that looked at the woman who made her own way into the house of Simon the Pharisee, and we explored the text that introduced the parable known as the Good Samaritan. Once a man said, "The gospel is asking me to ask myself a question. It is asking me to ask what I would want if I were a homosexual." I asked him what he thought his answer to this would be, and he said, "Love and protection." I asked groups who they thought the marginalized are in their society and they said, "Terrorists, homosexuals, and prostitutes."

We spoke about risk and one man said, in front of a group, "Pádraig, when in your life have you ever taken a risk?" It was a good question, and part of me would have loved to have told the truth. But I wasn't there for a risk. I was there with the phone number of the Irish embassy in my back pocket, a bag packed, a conveniently respelled name, an air ticket home, and a lot of chocolate. I barely slept, but the adrenaline was enough for a while.

In the Shelter

Hello to risks that are barely risks.

♦

On the last day of the trip, I was exhausted. I had been reading Wilfred Bion's writing about how hostility can manifest itself in groups, and I had found his words—although unsettling—helpful in giving me some tools to notice group dynamics as well as my own complicity. I was speaking with a group and one of them mentioned that their new readings of the Gospels made them question the way they thought about the upcoming Anti-Homosexuality Bill. One of the participants stood up, looked at me, and said, "This kind of conversation is illegal. It is illegal. It might be legal in America or other places, but it is illegal here." Coming from a participant who oftentimes had been a voice of inclusion, diversity, and subtlety, the underlying sense of power in his message was clear. While I was not surprised at the words, I realized that my own reserves of energy were depleted. What did surprise me, however, in the middle of this incident, was to realize that I had moved, unconsciously, closer to the door. I recognized not only my sense of fear but, much more importantly, the powerful sense of alert that I had. I was awake to every word used, keen to the hostility that seemed to be aching for a target.

♦

Hello to the powerful truth that the body tells.

♀

I relate this not because the events were particularly traumatic—after all, as I've said, I was booked to leave—but because it seems unlikely to me that among the dozens of people I interviewed that week there weren't other LGBT people. I've experienced enough homophobia in my life—homophobia that has affected my job, housing, safety, and mental health. But the day of that exchange I wondered who else I'd met who was living in the way that was so alert to the tiniest hint that they might be suspected of being LGBT.

I thought about the Irish missionaries of various denominations who have participated in endorsing such a didactic discursive climate. I wondered about what the hell Jesus would say if he were in that room and I wondered if I'd even want to recognize him. I wondered at my own complicity in all of this, and I praised those people in Uganda who use their voices to speak out the truth. I didn't go to visit LGBT organizations there because I didn't want to draw attention to people who may not have wanted attention drawn to them.

My guess, though, is that I encountered numbers of LGBT people who knew well to keep quiet. I wondered at the skills of survival they must practice on a daily basis, and I wondered about any preemptive practices they put in place to ensure safety from questioning. I wondered about the lies they had to tell—not only to others but to themselves—in order to entertain the possibility of living, and I wondered at the power, dignity, and imagination denied them in the name of God, Christian morality, and Ugandan sovereignty. And anyway, I felt that the law had more to do with rejecting self-appointed Western

233

interventions in Ugandan life than it had to do with hatred of LGBT people. The "help" that had been given Uganda in the decades since independence was spoken of more as a way of preserving indebtedness than supporting development in a post-colonial reality. Sometimes, underneath the scandal lies the understandable.

Fear and courage start off as the same sign when you speak with your hands.

♀

Hello to fear.

Hello to courage.

Hello to the underneath.

♀

I find myself convinced that Jesus of Nazareth, were he to be present among the Ugandan populace, would be found speaking with and about the moral capacity of lesbian, gay, bisexual, and transgender Ugandans. I imagine that they would be the moral actors in the stories he would tell. The controversy would not be whether he had Beelzebul in him—a diabolical name, and an accusation levied against him—but whether he himself was one of those moral abnormals.

The dignity of Samaritans was not argued by discussing the similarities and dissimilarities between the Samaritan and Judaean versions of the Torah. The question about difference was on the level of not only "who is right" but also "who is wrong." Note the pronoun here—it is the *who* that is right or wrong. And the *who* is always a person or a group, and if the person or the group is wrong, then all kinds of things can be justified in maintaining such a story. Jesus argued for dignity by highlighting examples and telling stories of courageous and moral Samaritans who did what was good when those who claim to be in the right group were not doing anything. The Gospel stories are the antidote to what Liechty and Clegg note. When we say, "You are a less adequate version of what we are," we are often willfully ignorant of our own perpetrations even while those who are the victims of our words are demonstrating courage, virtue, and graciousness.

Then, as now, the easiest way to silence those who wish to tell other stories is to shut them up, and not only to shut them up, but to disgrace their name before you shut them up.

A spirituality that cannot bear witness to itself in the face of power is not a spirituality that I am interested in. I have suffered enough, and caused enough suffering, to know that anything that is either beyond or within me needs to be tempered with a voice that can speak to power.

Hello to power.

There is an Irish phrase that I hesitate to use here because no proverb is adequate. But no language is ever adequate, so I might as well. *An t-ualach is mó ar an gcapall is míne*—the heaviest load is on the gentlest horse. I don't think that LGBT people are necessarily gentler, but I do think that the burden of survival often demands most from those whose survival is hardest. There is a diabolical kind of reciprocality in this—because those of us who have suffered are not indemnified from the possibility of causing suffering to others. We can pay it forward like the worst. That said, however, LGBT people know far too well that a spirituality in denial of the privilege inherent in abstract conversations about sexuality—the effects of which are anything but abstract on LGBT people—is spineless and couldn't carry a load, no matter how gentle.

What is clear from our human storytelling is that over and over the most powerful stories emerge from those who have survived the most powerful abdication of responsibility. Just because this is true doesn't mean we should depend on it.

Hello to the need to fucking change.

One story in Luke's Gospel is foundational for me. In this story, an anonymous woman makes her way to the home of Simon the Pharisee, where Jesus and some others are having a meal. Little information is given about the intention of Simon or the purpose of the meal. This woman—often incorrectly named as Mary Magdalene—enters the house and weeps at the feet of Jesus, wiping her tears away with her hair and anointing the feet of the Nazarene with ointment from a jar that she had brought with her.

It's helpful to notice the details of the text—Luke notes that the woman is *behind* Jesus, but she is touching his feet and wiping them with her hair, so it seems that he must have been reclining at a low table, most probably leaning on his left hand. In this way, his feet were not directly under him, but rather out to his side. The woman can be understood to be behind him, but not crouching under a chair.

The text is firmly located as part of Luke's ongoing process of establishing Jesus as a *new* kind of prophet, because the host in this small story, Simon, does not question how the woman came in, or how he can get her out. Rather, he questions whether Jesus could be a prophet if he's allowing himself to be anointed by such a woman with her reputation and bad name. So, in a way, she was a pawn in the game of judging whether Jesus was indeed a prophet or not. The identity of the pawn seems irrelevant in the mind of the host; it is the impact of association with such a one as this that is notable.

So a small exchange ensues—Jesus tells a parable about two people being forgiven debts and asks Simon a question, the answer to which was already obvious. Then he does something much more interesting. He turns to the woman and asks a question. Before the question is explored, it's worthwhile to pay attention to the body. He turns to the woman. To do this he would have had to incline his head away from his host—surely as insulting then as it would be now—and in so doing he creates the situation where the woman has two men looking in her direction. Or, at least, she has one man looking at her and another man looking at the man looking at her. Either way, rather than merely being the scandal upon which another's reputation is judged, she is now a focus. The question posed to Simon is simple: "Do you see this woman?"

I think the answer is clear. I think the answer is "No." I think the answer is that Simon does not see her, but he sees everything he thinks he sees about her: what he imagines about her name, what he imagines about her reputation, what he imagines about what she does. Each of these tells a story about Simon, not about her, but Simon's the one with power, so he's well able to direct attention away from the truth behind his own fears and fantasies.

Jesus speaks about her and honors her touch, her emotion, her gift, her kisses. He proclaims forgiveness to her—but as a response to, not a precursor for, her love. It seems that the story of the economy of love and forgiveness told by Jesus too has been moved by being turned toward her. She is not worthy of mere inclusion. She is the site of learning and change.

Do you see this woman? If not, what do you see between you and whoever it is you don't see?

♦

Hello to the question.

Hello to the lenses through which I peer, seeing more of my self than I do of my subject.

Hello to power.

♦

When the farmer from New Zealand—remember her? pages and pages ago?—found herself in the body of Simon the Pharisee watching the outpouring of love and grief and dedication and desperation with such jealousy, she offered a key to understanding a message in this text. It seems that Jesus responded most generously to people who were aware of their own need. To those who came knowing what they wanted and not playing games, Jesus's answers were at least straightforward, if not satisfactory. To those who came with agendas and traps, the engagement seems to be oriented toward the jugular of power. The premise of the question is often addressed, usually at the expense of its substance. The tone here seems to be that Simon cannot see an exchange such as the one unfolding in front of him without reevaluating the character of Jesus, a reevaluation that happens at the expense of Jesus's prophetic claims. However, this hostility is indicative of something deeper. What is it that Simon might have seen in the woman that required him to hide behind the thick lens of predictable judgment? Was it possible that he too was being invited to come to terms with his own needs, his own quest for meaning, his own small desperations and unforgiven corners? Whose reputation was he most concerned about? I don't think he was, finally, even that concerned about Jesus's reputation. It was his own reputation he was interested in, his own place in the halls of power, his own voice among the voices of the just.

Quietly now, greet the games of power we employ to tell us who we are.

Hello to the games of power.

In the Shelter

●

Jesus of Nazareth was not a powerless man. I do not believe that for a second. I don't even believe he played games of powerlessness, because those games are a luxury afforded to those whose agency is often unquestioned. I'm not very interested in lifestyles of chosen poverty, but I'm very interested in those who have been denied the possibility of a living wage. I believe Jesus knew exactly what he was doing, and he just used a different kind of power. When, in John's Gospel, I read about a woman being stoned, I see Jesus using power. He bent down and scribbled in the ground, writing words that we do not know. He did that, knowing—I am guessing—that many of those who were about to throw stones couldn't read the words even if they could have strained their necks to see them. He used his privilege to deflect attention, and in so doing he undid the story that held the slew of stoners together. This was not powerlessness. It was power and it is deep in us.

●

The woman was about to be stoned because of the addictions of the stoners. They were addicted to a violent kind of belonging, a kind of community that forges its borders through selective exclusion. She was about to be stoned with their bone-breaking morals that would prefer to kill a woman rather than examine their own complicity. We all need to be rescued from this kind of power—from both its appeal and its effect. An undoing of this power is seen when power is used for love. Power, used well, should be empowering, contagious, and creative. It should be collaborative, enabling, and protective. It should be self-critical, curious, and brave. It should know its own limits and be prepared to risk its own reputation. This kind of power asks questions to which it does not know the answers and listens because in listening is learning, and in learning is life.

Hello to the power of learning.

♀

Ira Byock is a palliative care doctor who has, in the course of his career, observed that people who are dying tend to say four things. They say, "Please forgive me"; they say, "I forgive you"; they say, "Thank you"; and they say, "I love you." Four small sentences made up of eleven smaller words. I am struck by the grounding counterpoint provided to the three questions of life—the whoamiwhereamigoingwhatamisupposedtodo questions. It is not as if the questions that agitate life are necessarily undone by Ira's observation of the statements that sum it up. But there is something valuable to note.

We move from questions about our own ontology as meaning-making, story-seeking individuals to statements or requests that are entirely predicated upon responsibility and reciprocality. The move from one to another demonstrates a substantial change in the question of "Who am I to be?"—a question that can trespass upon the quicksand of an ideology more concerned with its intention than its impact—to statements that recognize the truth of how we hurt and heal each other, of how very much we can mean to each other.

In the Shelter

Hello to apology.
Hello to thankfulness.
Hello to forgiveness.
Hello to love.

"Is áit an mac an saol," we say in Irish—"life is very strange." We create stories that protect an idea and use power to exclude or include based on the same idea. History has shown that no religious or social ideology is immune from the capacity to make its doors as sharp as they are open, branding those who enter or maiming those who leave. Part of this, I am convinced, is because we speak in singular terms. I am a person, and I have a faith, and I belong to a group. Surely by now we must know that we are plural. I am peoples, with faiths and belongings. I have capacities and incapacities, and my power too is plural, hopefully hurting less with years.

Hello to the power of belonging.
Hello to the responsibility of the power of belonging.

Returnings

I see her, former colleague
in the baggage area of a
foreign airport.

Oh hi, she says,
looking awkwardly toward the
empty carousel.

Then she decides.
I hear you're gay now, she says.
Are you still a Christian?

Oh how will we tell this story?

She, to her friends, with
sadness, curiosity and prayers
for reorientation and returning.

Me, to mine, with sadness,
anger and prayers for
refocusing the lenses and returning.

And the anger was all mine,
but that question
was all about her.

Should we not just dance instead?
I should have said,
together turn a little waltz in

the chorus of our own bodies
while we wait and wait and wait for something better
than the empty carousel of this question.

How will we tell this story?
How will I tell this story?
With sadness,

with practicings of little ballroom dances
while we wait, confidently,
for what is most important to be returned.

10

Hello to story

For more than a decade my favorite book has been Vikram Seth's *A Suitable Boy*. Every second year or so, I begin thinking about the characters and I start to miss them, so I read it again. It is—or at least was—the longest single-volume novel in the English language. The opening scene sets the tone: "'You too will marry a boy I choose,' said Mrs. Rupa Mehra firmly to her younger daughter."

I mostly read and reread the book because I love Mrs. Rupa Mehra so much. Mrs. Rupa Mehra is the widowed mother of four adult children, and she is the embodiment of India, motherhood, practicality, letter writing, vast handbags, love, and sentimentality. When the *Guardian* newspaper printed a review of the book, first published in 1993, it described it as being "vast and amiably peopled." Each time I read it, I am moved by the care with which Vikram Seth has written his characters. There are two round brothers who run a bookshop. They are not terribly important, but their bookshop is the site of an important meeting. So they are described for a page with kindness and curiosity. There is an unnamed woman on a train, but I'd recognize her if I saw her, and from time to time I hope that my own rhetoric could match that of Begum Abida

Khan, an erudite and fiery politician. The book is a family tree of story during a snapshot of India with intersecting lives affecting each other and sheltering each other. I bought it in an airport when I had a long journey ahead of me, and I've still got the copy I bought. After many moves and many readings, it's held together with tape and the corners of its pages are soft and curved. It is a book I have lived with and lived by. The stories of its characters, though fiction, echo the imagination and family of Vikram Seth, and now it is part of the story I tell about myself.

We are the stories we tell about ourselves and we are more than the stories we tell about ourselves. We fiction and fable our lives in order to tell of things that are more than true and we lie—if only by omission—by reducing ourselves to mere facts. "*Ní fiú scéal gan údar,*" we say in Irish—"there's no worth to a story without the teller." We create anxiety for ourselves by either rejecting or being limited only to the story of our lives. To live well is to see wisely and to see wisely is to tell stories and to tell stories is to tell of things that are always changing, because even if the stories don't change, the teller does, and so the story always moves.

Hello to the stories we tell.

♀

Wendy Farley is a theologian who, at the age of forty-one, lost the ability to read. At that time, she was freeing herself from a husband who had become a danger to her, and in the midst of that heavy story, her body, her eyes, her brain, or something decided that of all things to sacrifice, reading should be it. She continued to teach during that time—she needed the income—and she wrote her book *The Wounding and Healing of Desire* while she was unable to read. Most of the references in that book are to the folk songs she listened to during the time when, as she says, "the lights went out on my reading." She quotes bluegrass; Mary Black; Pema Chodron; Alison Krauss; *O Brother, Where Art Thou*; and Emmylou Harris.

It is as if her body decided that she had read enough and that she now needed to live from the wisdom she sang, the wisdom she listened to, and the uncategorized wisdom of memory and fable. She quotes great theologians, but from memory, not from citation. It is their flavor, not their purity, that influences her writing, and in so doing, she created a theology that is story and survival. It is unique, and while I wouldn't wish the experience on anyone, I am glad that she wrote, even while she couldn't read.

Hello to the stories we would never choose.

♀

The accepted sequence of New Testament books suggests that there is the story, and then there is the *commentary* on the story. As if to say the letters that follow the Gospels are the real meat of substance, epistles from important men to new Christian communities springing up all around the Mediterranean. But the writers of those letters seemed to know very little about the Gospels. Their letters focus mainly on the meaning of Jesus's life and the impact of both his death and resurrection in light of his identity. The woman who pushed through the crowd receives no commentary. No commentary either for the man of Gerasenes, the anonymous people who showed courage, Zacchaeus or the Syrophoenician woman whose double diminutive demanded the attention of Jesus.

The sequence of the books of the New Testament could, perhaps, be better arranged, putting the Epistles with their arguments and theories at the beginning, and moving toward the culmination of those letters—the Gospels, stories of the incarnated life that was not held by death. It wouldn't be perfect, but it'd suggest the truth that what began in theological commentary—early apostles writing about the theological impact of their belief in the life and death and resurrection of the Son of God—moved toward narrative. What began as proposition finds flesh in story.

Hello to the ideas that find flesh in story.

There are, of course, many stories of love and argument woven in and out of the Epistles. The salty lives of the early Christian communities are revealed through the praises and admonitions of the letters. But the incarnated flesh of Jesus of Nazareth takes form through the later gospel tradition. So story is not only the beginning point upon which later commentary rests, but story is the very essence of it all. Our culture sometimes implies that storytelling is a pastime for children, or those with short attention spans, but story is the multilayered world that presents many things all at once.

◉

"We do not tell stories as they are; we tell stories as we are." Who said that first? What's lovely is that it's not known. Some attribute it to Anaïs Nin but she, in *Seduction of the Minotaur*, has the character Lillian recall Talmudic words: "We do not see things as they are, we see them as we are." There's a long argument about whether those words are in the Talmud or not and another argument about the other authors who use the phrase. It's like a piece of wisdom that's been owned by many because we know it's more than the sum of its words. The stories we tell also tell us. They are mirrors that move and sometimes change, and sometimes they tell more than we wish they would.

So we borrow stories of fiction, we remember stories of survival, we read and we forget to read, we invent words that tell us who we really are, and we forget the places those words started. We think analysis is the inheritor of story, but all analysis leads back to story. We read books again and again and we tell stories in order to tell of things bigger than us.

Hello to story.

In 1936, Anton Boisen, a hospital chaplain, published the book *The Exploration of the Inner World: A Study of Mental Disorder and Religious Experience*. He didn't write his book from an outside perspective. He had taught French and German in the United States, and at the turn of the nineteenth into the twentieth century, he suffered the first of his psychotic episodes. He trained in theology and after the First World War lived through another breakdown during which he began to consider the importance of holding psychology and religion together.

In the Shelter

In his major book—a book both of its time and timeless—he coined the phrase "the living human document."

When I first read this, I began to relax. As a zealous teenager, I had grown anxious because somebody told me that because I loved stories and people, I therefore was lacking in love for God. Now it seems like a non sequitur, but at the time it formed the basis of a few months' anxiety. But even that was not fruitless because now it's a good story. I know that I tell a lot of stories. For me, it's the only way that life can become a verb. I cannot live more than the lives I lead, and so, through love and curiosity, eavesdropping and storylistening, I can live bits of the lives I don't. One-sentence stories, ten-sentence stories, well-told stories, choppy stories.

◉

When Tolkien wrote his own version of the story of the world, he spoke of it in terms of music. The One made his holy ones make music and they lived in unison and harmony. They—like harps, lutes, pipes, trumpets, and organs—began a great music, "endless interchanging melodies woven in harmony that passed beyond hearing into the depths and into the heights." This music and the echo of this music went to the void and the void was unvoiced.

Ovid tells the story differently. In the opening book of *Metamorphoses*, the story of the chaos is undone by a god—or, as Ted Hughes translates, "some such artist as resourceful"—who splits earth and sky, sea from land, and heavens from the air. Ovid tells the story that after the chaos was controlled, humankind emerged.

Hello to story

Like Genesis, Ovid suggests two origins of humanity: perhaps the humans were made by the worldmaking god or perhaps the newly born earth contained fragments of the skies fashioned into humans, in a reflection of the gods above.

Hello to the versions of the story of chaos.

Hello to the versions of the story of us.

♀

What does all this mean? It means that we are never finished telling stories, even telling the start of stories. One of the times I asked a group to write and tell the first sentence of the story of their lives, somebody wrote, "Not many people get born in an elevator," and another wrote, "What does it mean my 'waters have broken'?" In the same group, I asked people to name words they loved and people said *dragonfly*, *breath*, and *insouciant*. They named words they hated and they said *should*, *success*, and *y'know*. One person said they loved and hated the word *love*, and another said they loved and hated the word *freedom*.

A man in the room said he grew up in a cultureless place, but that he came alive when his English teacher used to read poetry. A woman said that when she was a child, her mother used to read Ovid's *Metamorphoses* to her in Latin. The child didn't understand it, but she knew her mother did. She used to stare at the Latin words and then stare at her mother and wonder if she was some kind of small god.

She was.

Hello to the words of the stories, words we hate and words we love.

In the Shelter

Sometimes a story only needs one word. I know a woman—Tanya Coburn—who writes stories and poems and teaches the art of listening. She tells the story of being a young woman traveling through Europe. It was the 1980s, and she met a man in Paris and, for the first time in her life, fell in love. They arranged to meet at an embassy in Rome a week later, and on the arranged day she went and waited at the embassy. Her lover did not show. She went again the next day and the next, but he never showed. She was devastated. She walked back to the place where she was staying, alone in a land where she did not speak the language. As she neared her temporary home, a young priest walked by her. She didn't know him and he didn't know her. He looked at her and said *coraggio*—courage. When Tanya told this story, she looked around the room and said that she has lived her life differently since the hearing of that word.

Hello to the story of a word.

We tell stories with words and we tell stories about words. A man said to me once, "I used to hate the word *cope*. Now I respect it."

Hello to the story of coping.

For years I had long hair. I got it cut short on a Friday so that I could get used to it over a quiet weekend. When I went to work on Monday, my friend Karen asked, "Well, were you long thinking about getting your hair cut or was it impulse?" I said I'd been planning it for ages, and she asked when I got it done, and I said, "Frid—" And she said,

> Only because my brother got his done in between Christmas and New Year, and my daddy, you see, he has long hair, been long since the eighties, or, dear God, nearly as long as I've been around, always had the long hair, longer than mine. And my brother—he's a Goth—and he had long hair, I'm his friend on Facebook, you see, and over the years it was purple, and shaved, and long, and up here, and around there, and my mummy, she cuts hair, she cuts her own mummy's hair—my granny, you know—and my granda's, and her own brother's too. So my brother, he comes down from his room over Christmas, and says to her, he says, "Cut my hair, would you, Mummy?" and she says, "Oh God, no, go to a stylist, son," and he says, "No, Mummy, you cut it," so she does, and she's crying because there's hair all over the floor, and I near died when I saw on Facebook that his hair's cut, but it's long on the front, and short on the back, so he piles it up. He's still a Goth, like, but, as I say, it's still a wee bit long in the front, and when I saw it on Facebook, dear God, maybe I should go get mine cut too, because my brother, well, as I said, he had his hair cut, and

my sister, last year, she got her hair cut, and well,
maybe I should get mine cut too.

In American Sign Language, there are two signs for story. The first places both open-palmed hands in a prayer position, only not quite touching. The palms are drawn apart and the thumb and index finger of each hand form little circles. It is as if to say that a story is made up of lots of little circles. Or I sometimes think it looks like curtains opening for a play. The other sign for story makes both flat hands, palms down, describe a stage and then repeat that slightly higher up. It is as if these signs are saying that stories open us to an experience where many small layers combine to make multistaged meanings. What I love about Karen's storytelling is that she reminds me of the writer of the Gospel of Matthew, the author of the book of generations, the library of lives loved, the collection of stories overlapping. She, like Matthew the evangelist, begins all of her stories by telling tales of surrounding and preceding lives.

◉

Hello to the long-winded interrupting story. It is vast and amiably peopled.

◉

Stories also have their limits, it must be said.

Hello to story

It is the *flaws* in the library of lives lived and loved that we most often live by. We hear stories of past lives and find ourselves marveling at how such fractured lives could have survived. We read things we wrote a year ago and wonder at how things have changed, or our own ignorance.

This is why I love old texts, especially texts like Scripture that have such complicated and shameful language. We read of abominations, and we read that Jesus said that God hates divorce, and we hear that demons were discerned where today we would diagnose something much less convenient, and we read of easy justification of war and simple declarations about the end of the world. To rid the Bible of these unfinished story lines would be to rid ourselves of our own unfinished story line. We must remember. We must bear witness. We must read the past as the unfinished story that keeps us changing.

Welcome to the changing story. It is never finished.

◊

It shocks me, sometimes, when I meet someone who knew me most when I was particularly sick. "How's your health?" they ask, and I reply, "Fine," and they say, "Really?" and then I remember. They knew me when I was steadying myself to walk. It is a relief to forget, and when I remember the relief, I remember to be grateful. There was a time when feeling ill was the first thing I thought about when I woke up, and now—I'm guessing by sheer luck—this is not the case. The story is sharp because where I find myself in good health, others do not. Stories can feel like oppression too. I heard of a woman whose son had been sick and, to the surprise of everyone, recovered. She stood to tell the story of his recovery at a church service on a Sunday morning. As she stood to tell her story of joy, she saw another woman whose son had died and she modified her words a little, to make its edges less sharp. She did not dampen her joy; she just dampened the thump of unshared fate.

Hello to the cruelty of stories with happy endings. They don't make everybody happy.

And yes, I know—I've told that one already. That's the way with stories, they are told and told and told.

Hello to the repeated story.

"We are more than our biography," John O'Donohue used to say. He recounted stories he'd heard from people who were bound by the tenses of the biographies they recited. "I am the product of my biography," somebody might say, and while he believed them he also wondered if they had conjugated the verb *to be* too solidly. He wondered whether there wasn't a part of them—perhaps a part they barely knew of—that held its own glorious independence from the experiences of their lives.

Jeanette Winterson says something similar when, in her memoir *Why Be Happy When You Could Be Normal?*, she writes, "When we tell a story we exercise control, but in such a way as to leave a gap, an opening. It is a version, but never the final one. And perhaps we hope that the silences will be heard by someone else, and the story can continue, can be retold. When we write we offer the silence as much as the story. Words are the part of silence that can be spoken."

Hello to the story that's never finally finished.

♀

Other times, it's wise timing that's needed. "*Ni hé lá na gaoithe lá na scolb*," we say in Irish—"a windy day is no day for thatching." At one point, in my midtwenties, I decided that now was the time to tell everyone that I was gay. Given my involvement in religious work, I knew my storytelling would likely evoke invasive questions, rearranged friendships, and polite insults. A few people knew already and those who knew knew that it was a story that still sat uneasily in me. One friend who could read my own anxiety—and my own flimsy confidence—said that I might want to wait until things were a bit more settled for me before telling stories to others that I could barely cope with myself. God, she was right.

When, a few years later, I did start telling stories, I met support, surprise, sincerity, and insult—polite and impolite. But what was different was that I was different. The reactions of others had less power over me to undo me. Not all stories need to be told all at one time, I suppose, is the wisdom that my friend's words gave me. But for every similitude, a dissimilitude is implied, and I find myself wondering at those for whom wise timing was never an option, as their stories were wrenched from them and they had no kind friend to speak supportive words.

Hello to the stories we control.

Hello to the stories that we have no control over.

The stories we live in, the stories we live by, and the stories we tell can, we hope, deepen our story of being alive. But they are uncontrollable. We have ideas about what our lives will be, but then control is taken from us, and we find ourselves in a story we did not choose.

Hello to the stories that shape us even though we didn't choose them.

For years, I have loved hearing stories of people's experiences in prayer. I suppose that all of these words are trying to describe the encounter between prayer, story, and the ordinary experiences of our lives. But prayer is often uncontrollable too. Often we tell the story of prayers that are like shots in the dark. But also, sometimes, without any map, we land on the right words in prayer.

Mark Jarman writes of a time when "half asleep in prayer I said the right thing." He knew it was the right thing because he felt a change in his body, as if somebody—and by this I always read "God"—had come into the room and he knew an overwhelming joy. He tried, over and over, to recall this experience, but he can't. He'd only said thanks and had an unexpected visitor. "Once was enough to be dissatisfied," he says of this kind of prayer, and I think I know what he means.

Hello to story

●

Hello to the story of prayer.

●

When I read Mark Jarman's words, I think of the few times when in a moment of prayer, I landed on the words that told me what I was most needing to hear. I once was in desperate need of making a decision and, almost without control, found myself marching to a small chapel. Inside, possessed with an agency I still marvel at, I asked myself what story of the Gospels most sounded like what I needed to hear. It was a question of pure intuition. On the whim of some kind of autopilot, I turned to the last chapter in John, the chapter where Peter has decided that he is returning to fishing and he goes, together with six others who follow him even if he may have wished they weren't. After a night of fishing—or, to be clear, a night of unsuccessful fishing—a sharp-eyed disciple spots someone on the shore and mentions to Peter that it is Jesus. Peter, who is stripped, puts clothes on and jumps into the sea, a strange reversal of the usual order of things. But it's also understandable. This is the man who had stood around a charcoal fire and told barefaced lies. He may have been reluctant to let such exposure be mirrored in his bare-arsed body. Gone too is the interest in waterwalking. Miracle isn't the purpose anymore; he now needs something much more important. The breakfast—for that is what it ends up being—is mostly eaten in silence. Afterward, Jesus, standing around a charcoal fire that he seems to have kindled himself, asks three questions about love. After he asks the third time whether Peter loves him, Peter says, "Lord, you know everything." I don't read this as a declaration of omniscience. I think he's saying, "I know you know I've fucked it up," and I think Jesus is saying, "Alleluia."

So anyway, there I was, in a haze, and I turned to this text. I was twenty and it felt like I had to make big decisions. I turned to this story and I felt like it read me. Not because any particular similitude was implied, but because I heard an echo of failure, an echo of confusion, and an echo of accompaniment. For twenty years, I've read this story on my birthday. We are old friends, now, me and this story, each growing and each changing. It means something different to me now than it did then, but I think it's a text I'll read until I end.

When I was younger, I thought this text meant I was going to become a priest. Then everything happened, and I've begun to live with the text rather than asking the text to live for me. I still read the story every year on my birthday.

Hello to the happy accident of the changing story.

I heard Carol Ann Duffy say recently that she thinks that if she believed in God, she would find prayer most consoling, because to pray is to believe that someone is listening. "For everybody else," she said, "there's poetry." I sat and thanked God, or whoever might be listening, for prayer and poetry.

One time, I was trying to pray, and without any rhyme or reason I found myself back in that awful, frightening cave from my dream— the cave I thought I was going to die in. But the cave was quiet now, and there was a soft gray light, and there was a sense that somewhere, instead of a chasm of fire, there was a pool of clear water. I have no idea what it meant, but for a moment it felt like a long, long time. I didn't just feel like my words were being listened to, it was my life—with its borders, shadows, and unfinished stories—that was gathered in an embrace of listening. In that experience, I was alone and not-alone there, there was something with me that felt, as Rumi says, closer to me than myself to myself. That there are only a few such stories in this half-lived life of prayer and decision-making that indicate the ordinary trend. Usually, I wake up tired and feel burdened by the decisions that don't make themselves and the tasks of the day that won't finish themselves.

Hello to the lists and the day and the tiredness and the coffee and the coffee.

Rumi also said to treat the body as a guesthouse. Each morning, he says, rather than lament the anticipated weights of the day, plan to entertain everything that comes like an honored guest in the house of the heart.

Hello to the day, and all it brings.

◉

Neither I nor the poets I love have found the keys to the kingdom of prayer, and we cannot force God to stumble over us where we sit.

But I know that it's a good idea to sit anyway. So every morning, I kneel, waiting, making friends with the habit of listening, hoping that I'm being listened to. There, I greet God and my own disorder. I say hello to chaos, my unmade decisions, my unmade bed, my desire, and my trouble. I say hello to distraction and privilege, I greet the day, and I greet my beloved and bewildering Jesus. I recognize and greet my burdens, my luck, my controlled and uncontrollable story. I greet my untold stories, my unfolding story, my unloved body, my own body. I greet the things I think will happen and I say hello to everything I do not know about the day. I greet my own small world and I hope that I can meet the bigger world that day. I greet my story and hope that I can forget my story during the day, and I hope that I can hear some stories and greet some surprising stories during the long day ahead. I greet God, and I greet the God who is more God than the God I greet.

Hello to you all, I say, as the sun rises above the chimneys of North Belfast.

Hello.

De Noche

By nighttime and streetlights,
I examine the light of the day
joined by the city's traffic sounds
coming through the window.

Asking where the heart
was buffeted and bolstered; what
little moment
held the unexpected moment;

the kindnesses received and the
kindnesses withheld;
the injustices perceived
and the focus on the self;

what small surprise
showed arrogance or assumption; nam-
-ing desolation and consolation
and all the little junctions of the day.

And then, at night, I make a promise
by the traffic and the streetlights, that
tomorrow, at the same time,
I'll meet the night again.

Hello to language

Postscript, five years later

This morning I woke up early. It's almost high summer; there's a hint of light in the sky all night long and the sunrise starts at around half past three. By the time I woke, about five, the sun was well up.

All these weeks in lockdown, I've been waking early. At the start, I was awake while it was dark and I'd take a blanket and sit outside on a chair and listen to the sounds of the dark—hares, birds, a small brown mouse snuffling around for any seeds the birds hadn't beaked up, an occasional car. I'd smell the dark too, that new scent at the end of the night. Earth and moss and dew.

I'd greet the day: hello to the dawn not yet here; hello to the hares mating in the field; hello to the new lambs, youngfooted tumbles of joy; hello to canceled work; hello to the saving balm of messages from friends; hello to COVID-19 death tolls from across countries: ten a day, fifty a day, a hundred, a thousand.

Hello to the bewilderment of pandemic.

In the early morning light I'd check on the midnight tulips I'd bought for Paul in Amsterdam. He'd planted them last winter. Now, spring, they have opened to their gorgeous beauty, a black purple, filled with light. The petals close at night and open early morning. If I managed to be up before the sun, I'd try to catch the tulips opening—but I never did. Hello to what won't let me see.

All around, these mornings, there was so much thriving: the young chaffinch would start up his mating song from the top of that one slender tree, and I'd listen to him sing and search and call and peal for mateship. Nature seeks a way to thrive: birds and viruses and hares and flowers.

Hello to the world. It is a strange place.

I love the word *secular*. When I was a teenager, I was introduced to a frightened form of religion that pitted spirituality against secularism. I'm older now, not saved by any god, but saved—sometimes—by language. Secular comes from old words: *seculer* and *saeculāris* meaning "of an age" or "occurring once in an age," from *saeculum* meaning "span of time." Secular echoes through the French word *siècle*. *Pour les siècles des siècles*, I said in French masses in Switzerland when I lived there as a young man—from century to century; forever and ever. Amen.

We have strange relationships with time—we are in it, and we imagine that what that means will last. Forever. And Ever.

Hello to the abominations of history.

Postscript, five years later

It has been such a consolation to arrive, finally, to a home in language. To be secular is to be in *this* age of *this* world. What a damned relief. When I think of the anxieties of my youth, I remember how worried I always was about the future—hell was always beckoning, and heaven was a dangling carrot to tempt me toward heterosexuality or celibacy. All along an actual saving call was coming from *now*, from *here*, from *this*, from *look*, from *everything all around*, from *see*, from *taste*, from *feel*, from *hello*, the hells in it and the little song of the *o*.

Hello to hello.

♀

Anyway, this morning I woke up. 5 a.m. The sun had been up for ages; everything was bright. Not everything that glitters is gold. Suns shine on sorry days too. A few weeks ago, a friend died suddenly. And so these mornings the first thing I say on waking makes no sense. Glenn's still dead.

Even though I know he's dead. I still need to be reminded. I need language and time to do their slow repetitive work.

After he died, I wept for a week. Then the shock lifted; I realized I barely believe he's dead. Hence my need to repeat over and over: *dead, dead, dead,* until it sounds like a sound that an animal would make, or a dull percussion: *dedd dedd dedd dedd dedd. Death* sounds different from *dead* in the mouth, because of that soft *th*, that voiceless dental fricative. *Th* like breath, or wealth, or bath, or filth. Abstract death's *th* softens the dead end of the particular in *dead*.

In the Shelter

Then I make tea. And have a banana. And read some poetry. And think about the day. Hello to it all, I've tried to say, but this death has knocked the breath out of me. I'm finding so many damned ways to avoid saying

goodbye.

◉

And I'm back with Tolkien's Elves again. Gandalf's death was too much for Legolas to translate. It was a matter for tears and not yet for song.

◉

Spirituality and secularism aren't opposites. When I was thinking of becoming a priest, people in the know would say, "Oh, a religious or a secular?" By that they were asking whether I meant to join an order of priests who live together in a monastery—like Franciscans, or Benedictines—or be a priest living and working in the world. To be present in the world is to be secular. To be alive is to be secular. Even if you only see woods and lakes and the inside of chapels; it's still the world. At the start of COVID, I was warned I was particularly at risk because I have chronic asthma. Struggling with breath means I think a lot about breathing. Breathing, from *spirare*, where the words *spirit* and *inspired* and *aspirate* all come from. The secular is not the opposite of the spiritual. The opposite of spiritual is suffocation.

Postscript, five years later

○

Hello to breath. Hello to staying alive.

○

I've been thinking, too, of the feelings of grief in the body. These last weeks while I've been crying, I've noticed that I clench and unclench my stomach. Or, maybe I should say that my stomach clenches and unclenches; I'm not sure who's doing it. I've noticed that I bow my head. I've noticed that I cover my face with my hands. I've noticed that my eyes feel hot before I cry. I've noticed that I give in to the full sound of crying when I believe nobody will hear. All that breath raking in and out of my body. At one point last week, I was standing in the kitchen pounding and kicking the door, howling at the feeling of loss like this was a first grief. Thank Christ nobody was around.

Breath does so many strange things to us.

○

When I was in therapy twenty years ago, I knew nothing about my therapist. One day I got a message to say that my appointments were canceled for a few weeks. When they resumed, I asked what had been up. My therapist paused, and then said, "My mother died. How have your weeks been?" As it happens they'd been awful—I look back now and think how exhausting I found everything—and as we got to the end of the session the therapist said, "In my grief, I can hear your own grief. I have someone to mourn. But you don't. And still you mourn. What's that about?"

I was shocked because this was one of the first times—and subsequently, one of the only times—the therapist had said anything personal. He was that kind of therapist: detached, determined that I'd learn to get approval for myself from myself and not anybody else. He believed in the awful lessons of loneliness.

A door had opened in him because of his mother's death. And from that door he looked out and saw that all along, I'd been in grief too. For some kind of death that I hadn't been able to put language to. *Language*, in Irish, is teanga, the same as the word for "tongue."

Hello to all the tongueless things.

♀

I did interviews about *In the Shelter* on its release. *You tell so many stories, little patchworks, it's unusual, it's very unusual. It. Is. So. Unusual.*, one interviewer said. He hated it. Someone else said, *I loved your autobiography*. Someone else was upset. Someone else said, *What is it? I don't really know.*

Last year a man named Samuel told me it was a long letter about how I've been saved by lines from books and poetry: sometimes holy, sometimes not. *You're not center stage*, Samuel said, *I think the point is language.*

I could have kissed him.

Hello to other people telling me the things I couldn't see.

Postscript, five years later

The project of language is a project of shaping tongues—or hands, or ink, or fingers, or bodies—around meaning. To make a noise, to say I am here, to find an echo and a shelter in another, to distinguish, to achieve, to learn, to grow. For a long time I thought the end point of all this was God. Now I wouldn't use that language; it was culpable of too much complicity and laziness and abdication for me. It's exciting to learn a changing language, to change a learning language.

Is this a book about what it's like to be lost? or found? someone asked me. *Mu*, I said. And, *Yes*. And I wonder again about getting that tattoo: not all who wander are lost.

♀

Hello to language.

♀

I keep trying to improve my Irish. Speaking it, thinking in it, writing in it. I have inherited self consciousness and perfectionism: so I am hesitant about the language when I know I'm going to make a mistake. The demise of the Irish language is a long story, but one thread of that story is that subjugation is always built on language: make a people influent in the language of power, and they'll be backfooted in negotiations. So language is politics and politics is languaged. To read is a moral act, I find.

Hello to reading.

271

In the Shelter

This morning, after reminding myself that my friend was still dead, I read. I read a Lorna Goodison poem about old colonizers. In it—the magnificently titled "Reporting Back to Queen Isabella"—Christopher Columbus, that Italian, is reporting to the Spanish queen about the country of Xamaica. X marks the spot in those old treasure maps, and he seemed to think the X of this island made it his. His report to the queen details everything he's seen there—the topography, the lush landscape, the rivers that his men had counted and numbered individually, the resources that he saw:

> . . . Overabundance of wood, over one hundred
> rivers, food, and fat pastures for Spanish horses, men,
> and cattle; and yes, your majesty, there were some people.

His seeing wasn't seeing. His seeing was "discovering." And his discovering became ownership. As if the Taíno hadn't already had their own relationship to the land that they lived on, the land they'd named Xamaica—land of wood and water. Or I've heard it another way too: great spirit of the land of man.

The poem isn't about Jamaica, though, or—at least—I don't read it as being about Jamaica. I read the poem as critiquing the European gaze on what is considered *new*. *New World*, some spin doctor came up with, thereby making it up for grabs, as if it had sprung, uninhabited by civilized or sophisticated peoples, fresh from the tongues of God.

Postscript, five years later

In Lorna Goodison's poem, she demonstrates that for Columbus, and the court of Queen Isabella, people are an afterthought; the final word in a poem that's more about robbery than discovery.

Europe is revealed in this poem.

Europe is revealed in many of Europe's projects; we like to pretend it's not but it is. "Those *Americans* and their racism," I hear Irish, English, Scottish, and Welsh people say, as if we didn't farm stolen land, forcing enslaved people to do work on that same land. I've heard American renditions of old Irish laments for how land was grabbed from us Irish by the English. Who brought those songs to America? Did they steal land? Did they enslave? Yes and yes. Yes.

Hello to the yes of facing history.

The population of Ireland at the start of the 1845–48 famine was over nine million. By 1848 the population was down two million: a million died and a million left, many to America. And there—ah, repeated horror—we often did unto others what was done unto us, and worse. And still. And here in Ireland too: this week, I heard one Black Irishman speak in perfect, gorgeous fluent Irish about the messages he's been given since he was young about how he isn't Irish. Not proper.

In 1845, at the start of the famine, Frederick Douglass had visited Ireland. His words to us were considered and generous. In the ensuing years, with ships of starving Irish people landing at the ports of America, the actions and words of the Irish were anything but.

In 1853, Frederick Douglass wrote:

In the Shelter

The Irish, who at home readily sympathize with the
oppressed everywhere, are instantly taught when they
step upon our soil to hate and despise the negro.
They are taught to believe that he eats the bread that
belongs to them. Sir, the Irish-American will find out
his mistake one day. He will find that in assuming
our avocation, he has also assumed our degradation.

Hello to the things of the past that we'd rather deny.
Hello to the language we need to tell them.

I try to read artists who have been denied a place in any canon. Irish
women were prevented from learning to write, Nuala Ní Dhomhnaill says, in order to prevent their keening laments from being
written down and thus entering the halls of poets. So the choice
of artists is always a political, ethical, and moral choice. The so-
called canon of poetry stretching back through the centuries is
overwhelmingly populated with men who look like me. Is that
because men who look like me tend to like poetry? Poetry happens
in the mouths of all. It has been the European project to steal the
world and make its structures in our image. It is the work of justice
to resist that project. Along the way I am hoping to change, I am
hoping to be less of a bastard, and I am hoping that I—and my

fellow white people—can practice a whiteness that upsets Eugene
O'Neill's prophesy:

> There is no present or future—only the past, hap-
> pening over and over again—now.

●

Hello to naming my complicity.

●

Conflict takes as long to deescalate as it took to escalate, I tell my
English friends on a regular basis, asking them to educate themselves
about the presence of English people and the English language in
Ireland for the past seven hundred years. I tell it to my straight
friends too. If I can say that to other powers, I need to say it to my
own powers, otherwise I'm a failure and a coward.

●

Hello to the long work.

●

Today I worked: a lecture given online, a poem polished, the scraps
of language assembled for an elegy for Glenn. I waded through

emails and offered apologies to people who'd been waiting while I wept for a week. I did the things any worker does. A publisher decided against a piece I'd written. Some sadnesses are easily ignored in light of other sadnesses. I'd written a piece about a friend, and while I won't publish it, I sent it to other friends. They rejoiced in the memory. It's done its work.

During breaks today, I'd look out to the field. Six weeks ago the field was filled with lambs whose madness made me think of Hopkins's line, *all this juice and all this joy*. Now they are already thickening with meat and solidity. They stand stiller now. I watched them while the kettle boiled. More tea. Peppermint and licorice.

Everywhere around me I see age. I wrote *In the Shelter* in my late thirties. I'm forty-five now. I feel like I've turned a corner, but God, I hate that phrase. Everything's a fucking journey, even though I despise that overused term. The future became less abstract for me when I turned forty. My thirties had been as fast and slow as any decade. So at forty, I looked ahead to fifty and sixty and seventy. Old wasn't Old anymore. It was now.

Hello to Time. Hello to all its languages.

♀

It's late. The sun goes down after 10 p.m. this time of year, and the light lasts longer. In the evening—if I'm in a good rhythm—I think about the day that's coming. I think about the things I am most looking forward to, especially the things I imagine will be a balm. And I distance myself from those things. Not to prepare for disaster or disappointment, but just to remove a bit of power from the things that I think will give me comfort. That way, if they comfort, then it's a delight, but not a demand. And something dreaded might not be so dreaded. Or it might be. It's a little bit Zen, it's a little bit Ignatian. It's a little bit rock 'n' roll too, because art can come from shock. It borrows from cynicism but isn't cynical. It knows that shocks might come, and hopes for the fortitude to be brave in the face of shocks, kind in the face of need, clear in the face of lies, steadfast in the face of denial, truthful in the face of falsehood.

Tomorrow, I will wake early, because I always wake early. I will take a breath—oh luxury to anticipate breath—and think about power when I speak. I will remind myself that Glenn is dead. I will make tea. I will read. There are currently forty books of poetry waiting. I will make that phone call I've been putting off for months. I will do it early so as not to waste more time. I will eat soup. I will work for my crust. I will say hello to the day as the day unfolds. And I'll say thanks. I will thank anyone who shares language with me tomorrow, in spoken or in written or in shouted forms. I will thank any language—old and new—that offers little lifeboats for me to be true. It is the one thing that saves me, even when I'm lost.

The One Thing

There must have been some other me, who
lived some other time, who realized he
knew the one thing that would save me.

And he must have found a little window,
opened it—and shouted through it—
that saving sound that saved me.

And he must have felt a failure, I am sure,
that other me, because he failed, he did, he didn't
save me from the other things that beat me.

And he must have sat, like some sad god
from sadder scriptures, and wept at all
he failed to do: he had so little time. And

all my life, I've been climbing up to
little windows—opening them—and saying
the one thing I can say: thank you.

Notes

Introduction and opening quotes

Diane K. Osbon, *Reflections on the Art of Living: A Joseph Campbell Companion* (New York: HarperCollins, 1991).

Annie Dillard, *The Writing Life* (New York: Harper & Row, 1989).

Legolas's reluctance to translate the laments for Gandalf comes at the end of the "Mirror of Galadriel" chapter, in *The Lord of the Rings* (New York: HarperCollins, 1995).

A fairly constant companion of mine is the *Chambers Dictionary of Etymology*, edited by Robert K. Barnhart and Sol Steinmetz, 3rd ed. (1999; London: Chambers, 2010). All my etymological musings come from this book. For any clumsiness, blame me, not this magnificent tome.

"Narrative Theology # 1" by Pádraig Ó Tuama is published in *Readings from the Book of Exile* (London: Canterbury Press, 2012).

1. Hello to here

J. R. R. Tolkien's words about escape were originally included as part of an Andrew Lang Lecture at the University of St Andrews on March 8, 1939. It was republished with minor alterations in *Tree and Leaf* (Boston: Houghton Mifflin, 1965).

David Wagoner, "Lost," in *Collected Poems, 1956–1976* (Bloomington: Indiana University Press, 1976).

I have tried, unsuccessfully, to locate the particular *National Geographic* article. However, I am fairly convinced that if I do, I will find that I have invented half of these details.

Merry and Pippin's encounter with Treebeard, the Ent, is found in Tolkien, *Lord of the Rings*, book 3, chapter 4.

Jane Kenyon, excerpt from "The Suitor" from *Collected Poems*, copyright © 2005 by The Estate of Jane Kenyon. Reprinted with the permission of The Permissions Company, Inc., on behalf of Graywolf Press (Minneapolis), www.graywolfpress.org.

My recollection is that the Henri Nouwen book that was mentioned was the wonderful *The Road to Daybreak*.

There are many introductions to Ignatius of Loyola's life and spirituality. The best way to encounter his methods of prayer is to engage with a trained spiritual director. The Spiritual Exercises are something to be engaged with, not learned or read about.

Tony Hoagland, excerpt from "Grammar" from *Donkey Gospel*, copyright © 1998 by Tony Hoagland. Reprinted with permission of The Permissions Company, Inc., on behalf of Graywolf Press (Minneapolis), www.graywolfpress.org.

2. Hello to the beginning

The midrashic discussions about the letters *A* and *B* are found across numerous texts. These quotes come from Jacob Neusner's magnificent book *Confronting Creation: How Judaism Reads Genesis* (Columbia: University of South Carolina Press, 1991), 39, 41. For further reading, see Raphael Posner and Wilfred Shuchat's *The Creation according to the Midrash Rabbah* (New York: Devora Publishing, 2002) and the midrashic text the Genesis Rabbah, found at sacred-texts.com/jud/mhl/mhl05.htm. Used with permission.

Phyllis Trible, *God and the Rhetoric of Sexuality* (Minneapolis: Fortress Press, 1978).

Notes

The reference for the opening quotes from the Gospel of Luke are Luke 1:1–4 and 5.

The quotes from the story of the lost boy Jesus come from Luke 2:49 and Luke 2:52.

The theologian who reflected on Mary and Joseph's need to forgive the child Jesus is David Tombs, the Howard Paterson Professor of Theology and Public Issues at the University of Otago in Aotearoa / New Zealand.

Avivah Gottlieb Zornberg, *The Murmuring Deep: Reflections on the Biblical Unconscious* (New York: Schocken Books, 2009).

Meg Kearney's quote about poets who borrow comes from the poem "Creed," in her book *An Unkindness of Ravens: Poems* (Rochester, NY: BOA Editions, 2001). She is referring to a quote by T. S. Eliot found in *The Sacred Wood: Essays on Poetry and Criticism* (New York: Barnes & Noble, 1960); he in turn had been referring to words of criticism published in an article by W. H. Davenport Adams, "Imitators and Plagiarists" (part 2 of 2), *The Gentleman's Magazine* 272 (1892): 613–28.

Elizabeth Bowen's quote is found in *The Heat of the Day* (New York: Alfred A. Knopf, 1949) and is cited in Christian Wiman's extraordinary memoir, *My Bright Abyss* (New York: Farrar, Straus and Giroux, 2013).

There are many versions of the text for the Shaker song. This one was sourced in a 1950 article by John M. Anderson, "Force and Form: The Shaker Intuition of Simplicity," *Journal of Religion* 30, no. 4: 256–60.

The quotes from the beginning of the Gospel of John are from the Contemporary English Version, copyright © 1991, 1992, 1995 by American Bible Society. Used by Permission.

Ben Marcus, *The Anchor Book of New American Short Stories* (New York: Anchor Books, 2004).

I guessed that the woman in England who spoke of "wild and precious" was making reference to the Mary Oliver Poem "The Summer Day." When I asked, she insisted she wasn't and wondered who Mary Oliver was. "Is she a friend of yours?" she asked.

Jane Austen, *Pride and Prejudice*, chapter 56. First published by Thomas Egerton (London, 1813).

Andrew Solomon's book *Far from the Tree: Parents, Children and the Search for Identity* (New York: Scribner, 2012) is an extraordinary exploration of humanity, diversity, and relationship. As soon as I finished it, I turned, again, to the first page.

The Samuel Johnson and Maya Angelou quotes come from Stedman Graham's book *Diversity: Leaders Not Labels* (New York: Free Press, 2006).

I use Martin Sternberg's *American Sign Language Dictionary* (New York: Harper Perennial, 1998) and David Brien's *Dictionary of British Sign Language/English* (London: Faber & Faber, 1992).

For more analysis of the historical context of the story of the Gerasene, see Adela Yarbro Collins, *Mark: A Commentary* (Minneapolis: Fortress Press, 2007) and Gerd Theissen, *The Gospels in Context: Social and Political History in the Synoptic Tradition* (Minneapolis: Fortress Press, 1991).

These words of Gollum's are found in *The Lord of the Rings. The Return of the King: Best Adapted Screenplay*, by Fran Walsh, Philippa Boyens, Peter Jackson, and J. R. R. Tolkien (Berlin: Cinemarket, 2003).

James Alison, *Faith beyond Resentment: Fragments Catholic and Gay* (New York: Crossroad, 2001). In this text, James Alison credits René Girard for much of the reasoning behind his own exploration of Mark 5. See Girard, *The Scapegoat* (Baltimore: Johns Hopkins University Press, 1986).

3. Hello to the imagination

Carl Jung, "Introduction to the Religious and Psychological Problems of Alchemy," in *The Essential Jung: Selected and Introduced by Anthony Storr* (Princeton, NJ: Princeton University Press, 2013).

The De La Salle Pastoral Centre in Belfast can be found at www.delasalleretreat .org.

Notes

Mary Terese Donze, *In My Heart Room: 21 Love Prayers for Children* (Liguori, MO: Liguori Publications, 1998).

The words about practical theology come from Elaine Graham in *Making the Difference: Gender, Personhood, and Theology* (Minneapolis: Fortress Press, 1996).

Declan Kiberd, *Inventing Ireland: The Literature of a Modern Nation* (Cambridge, MA: Harvard University Press, 1996).

The quote from *De Profundis* can be found in Oscar Wilde, *The Picture of Dorian Gray; De Profundis* (New York: Modern Library, 1926).

Julie Perrin (tellingwords.com.au) is a storyteller based in Melbourne, Australia.

The question from Romans is a paraphrase of 8:31.

Peter Rollins, *How (Not) to Speak of God* (London: SPCK, 2006).

4. Hello to trouble

Parts of this chapter appeared in "Shadows and Shelters in Belfast" in *Thresholds*, the spirituality and pastoral care journal of the British Association for Counselling and Psychotherapy (Spring 2014): 20–23.

Carl Jung, *Memories, Dreams, Reflections* (London: Fontana Press, 1995).

Bloodaxe has published a magnificent collection of Micheal O Siadhail's *Collected Poems* (South Park, Northumberland: Bloodaxe Books, 2013).

The poem "[the] north[ern] [of] ireland" is found in *Sorry for Your Troubles* (London: Canterbury Press, 2013).

The Leonard Cohen poem about falling is number 8 in Cohen's *Book of Mercy* (New York: Villard Books, 1984).

The Corrymeela Community was founded in 1965 by Ray Davey. It is a Christian witness to peace based in Northern Ireland (www.corrymeela.org).

Jonny McEwen designed the street project with Paul Hutchinson. Together, and with some others, they form ThinkBucket (thinkbucketblog.wordpress.com).

Olivia O'Leary's words were delivered during the *Ceiliúradh* on April 10, 2014, which was part of the Irish president's state visit to Britain.

"In the name" was originally published, in a different version, in *Discovering the Spirit in the City*, edited by Andrew Walker and Aaron Kennedy (London: Continuum, 2010).

5. Hello to what we cannot know

Robert M. Pirsig, *Zen and the Art of Motorcycle Maintenance: An Inquiry into Values* (New York: William Morrow, 1974). The quote about *mu* is on page 323.

Oscar Wilde, *The Importance of Being Earnest; a Serious Comedy for Trivial People* (1898), act 1.

Augustine of Hippo, *De doctrina Christiana*, book 1, 40.

Arundhati Roy's essay "Come September" is published in *The Algebra of Infinite Justice* (London: Flamingo, 2002).

Paul Monette, *Becoming a Man: Half a Life Story* (London: Abacus, 1994).

Nuala O'Faolain, *Are You Somebody? The Accidental Memoir of a Dublin Woman* (Dublin: New Island Books, 1997). The interview between Marian Finucane and Nuala O'Faolain was broadcast on RTÉ radio on April 12, 2008 (https://www.rte.ie/news/player/2020/0103/21683410 -marian-finucanes-iconic-interview-with-nuala-o-faolain/.)

The reference to Zornberg's book is from the already cited *The Murmuring Deep*, with this discussion being on page 68.

Stewart Henderson, *Homeland* (London: Hodder & Stoughton, 1993). Reproduced by permission of the publisher Hodder and Stoughton Limited.

"Narrative Theology # 2" was originally published in *Readings from the Book of Exile* (London: Canterbury Press, 2012).

6. Hello to the body

Carol Ann Duffy, *The World's Wife: Poems* (New York: Picador, 2000), copyright © Carol Ann Duffy, 2000.

The storytelling event is called Tenx9 (ten-by-nine), where nine people have up to ten minutes each to tell a real story from their lives (www.tenx9.com).

Augustine's words about Hope and her daughters are quoted in Robert McAfee Brown's magnificent book *Spirituality and Liberation: Overcoming the Great Fallacy* (Louisville, KY: Westminster John Knox Press, 1988).

For further reading on understanding Jesus's Jewish identity, Amy-Jill Levine's scholarship is a source of treasure and insight. See Amy-Jill Levine, *The Misunderstood Jew: The Church and the Scandal of the Jewish Jesus* (San Francisco: HarperSanFrancisco, 2006); see also Amy-Jill Levine and Marc Zvi Brettler, *The Jewish Annotated New Testament: New Revised Standard Version Bible Translation* (New York: Oxford University Press, 2011).

Kenneth E. Bailey, *Jesus through Middle Eastern Eyes: Cultural Studies in the Gospels* (Downers Grove, IL: IVP Academic, 2008).

The excerpt from the fields of Cormallen is from *The Lord of the Rings*, book 6, chapter 4.

The "Bearhug" poem is in Michael Ondaatje's collection *The Cinnamon Peeler: Selected Poems* (New York: Alfred A. Knopf, 1991).

The story starts with Acts 8:27, and quotations are taken from the ESV® Bible (The Holy Bible, English Standard Version®), copyright © 2001 by Crossway, a publishing ministry of Good News Publishers. Used by permission. All rights reserved.

The injunction regarding men who had been castrated taking part in the assembly is found in Deuteronomy 23:1, and the promise is found at Isaiah 56:5–6.

For instances of "touch" in the Gospel of Mark, see Mark 1:31, 41; 3:1–5; 5:23, 42; 6:2, 5; 7:32; 8:25, 32; 9:27; 10:16; and 14:46.

7. Hello to the shadow

The opening quote is from Genesis 3:8–11.

The quote from the start of the story of Cain and Abel comes from Genesis 4:1–7.

"Having Confessed" by Patrick Kavanagh, in *Collected Poems* (New York: W. W. Norton, 2004). For a masterful analysis of Kavanagh's religious poetry, see Tom Stack's book *No Earthly Estate: God and Patrick Kavanagh: An Anthology* (Dublin: Columba Press, 2002).

James Alison's quote about sin being an addiction is from his essay "Blind-sided by God," originally delivered at a conference in Trinity College Dublin in 2006. The full text is available on his website (www.jamesalison.co.uk).

Frederick Buechner, *Wishful Thinking: A Theological ABC* (New York: Harper & Row, 1973).

"Me" by Spike Milligan, in *Hidden Words: Collected Poems* (London: Michael Joseph, 1993).

Emily Dickinson's poem about Hope is #314. Emily Dickinson, *Poems by Emily Dickinson* (Second Series), ed. Thomas Wentworth Higginson and Mabel Loomis Todd (1891).

Adam Phillips, *One Way and Another: New and Selected Essays* (London: Hamish Hamilton, 2013).

Isaiah 55:2–13 was the Bible passage; the song is *You Shall Go out with Joy* by Steffi G. Rubin and Stuart Dauermann. Music and Lyrics Copyright © 1975 Lillenaus Publishing Company. Administered by CopyCare P.O. Box 77, Hailsham BN27 3EF, UK. music@copycare.com.

Emily Dickinson's poem "'Hope' Is the Thing with Feathers" is partially quoted here from the original editions released shortly after her death. The full poem has an additional stanza.

"10.30 a.m. Mass, 16 June 1985," by Paul Durcan, in *A Snail in My Prime: New and Selected Poems* (London: Harvill, 1993).

8. Hello to change

The April 11, 1963, edition of *New Scientist* carried the article "The Search for Perfect Numbers" by N. T. Gridgeman, which explores prime numbers beautifully. Demonstrating an echoing love for elegant numbers, Ira Glass's *This American Life*—a weekly radio show from Chicago Public Media—included a story about Frank Nelson Cole on the episode first broadcast on November 11, 2011.

Jane Austen's "Letter to Cassandra, January 24, 1813" is found in the wonderful book compiled and introduced by Deirdre Le Faye, *Jane Austen's Letters* (New York: Oxford University Press, 1995).

References to Jesus's temptation in the desert are found in Matthew 4:1–11, Luke 4:1–13, and briefly in Mark 1:12–13.

Si Smith has done an extraordinary series of images to accompany a reflection on the temptations of Jesus in the desert. In it, the devil appears to Jesus as a different shade of himself. It lends such new insight into these texts. These images, under the title "40," can be found on https://www.youtube.com/watch?v=P-6a25Yo2wE.

The Snoopy cartoon was published by Charles M. Schulz on August 9, 1976. See Charles M. Schulz, *The Complete Peanuts,* vol. 13, *1975–1976* (London: Canongate, 2013).

The interaction between Jesus and the Syrophoenician woman is found in Mark 7:24–30. It is also recorded, in a different form, in Matthew 15:21–28.

9. Hello to power

Joseph Liechty and Cecelia Clegg, *Moving beyond Sectarianism: Religion, Conflict, and Reconciliation in Northern Ireland* (Dublin: Columba Press, 2001).

Notes

The Lord of the Rings, book 5, chapter 2.

In particular, see *Dominus Iesus*, §16 and §17 at www.vatican.va.

William Carlos Williams, from *The Collected Poems: Volume I, 1909–1939*, copyright © 1938 by New Directions Publishing Corp. Reprinted by permission of New Directions Publishing Corp.

The quote about "mercenary reasons" comes from the Ugandan president Museveni's letter regarding the "Homosexual Bill," December 28, 2013.

Wilfred Bion, *Experiences in Groups: And Other Papers* (London: Routledge, 2010).

The story about the woman who makes her way into the home of Simon the Pharisee is found in Luke 7:36–50, and the story about the woman who was about to be stoned is found in John 8:2–11.

Ira Byock, *The Four Things That Matter Most: A Book about Living* (New York: Free Press, 2004). For a rich and spacious interview with Byock, search for his interview with Krista Tippett on the radio program *On Being* (www.onbeing.org). While there, listen to every episode of this magnificent program.

10. Hello to story

Vikram Seth, *A Suitable Boy* (London: Phoenix House, 1993). Seth is known for writing people of his acquaintance—friends and family—into the characters in his books. His 2006 book, *Two Lives* (London: Abacus, 2006), outlines some of the familial stories that weave their way into his fiction.

Wendy Farley, *The Wounding and Healing of Desire: Weaving Heaven and Earth* (Louisville, KY: Westminster John Knox Press, 2005).

Anaïs Nin, *Seduction of the Minotaur* (Athens, OH: Swallow Press, 1961). Garson O'Toole has recently published a fine exploration of the many possible origins of this phrase on his website (quoteinvestigator.com).

Notes

Anton T. Boisen, *The Exploration of the Inner World: A Study of Mental Disorder and Religious Experience* (New York: Willett, Clark, 1936).

J. R. R. Tolkien and Christopher Tolkien, *The Silmarillion* (Crows Nest, Australia: Allen & Unwin, 1977).

Ovid, *Metamorphoses*, book 1. There are many translations of Ovid. Ted Hughes's translation of twenty-four of the tales is magnificent: *Tales from Ovid* (New York: Farrar, Straus and Giroux, 1997).

The woman at the center of the *coraggio* story, Tanya Coburn, tells her own stories far better than I. Details of her published work are found at www.tanyacoburn.org.

I heard John O'Donohue mention the words "We are more than our biography" at a number of live events in the eighteen months leading up to his death. He discusses this concept in the interview "Inner Landscape of Beauty" on Krista Tippett's radio program *On Being* and also mentions it at a number of talks at the irreplaceable Greenbelt Festival—the full audio of which is available free by searching www.greenbelt.org.uk.

Jeanette Winterson, *Why Be Happy When You Could Be Normal?* (New York: Vintage, 2012).

Mark Jarman, "Unholy Sonnet, no. 11," in *Bone Fires: New and Selected Poems*, copyright © 1997, 2011 by Mark Jarman. Reprinted with permission of The Permissions Company, Inc., on behalf of Sarabande Books, www.sarabandebooks.org.

These words from Carol Ann Duffy were delivered during a recital at the Bloxham Festival of Faith and Literature in 2014 (www.bloxhamfaithandliterature.co.uk). Following this, she recited my favorite of her poems, the sonnet "Prayer," from *Mean Time* (London: Anvil Press Poetry, 1993).

The Rumi references are from the poems "A Thief in the Night" and "The Guesthouse," published in Jalāl al-Dīn Rūmī and Kabir Edmund Helminski, *The Rumi Collection: An Anthology of Translations of Mevlâna Jalâluddin Rumi* (Boulder, CO: Shambhala, 2005).

Hello to language: Postscript, five years later

The midnight tulips were bought in Amsterdam at a florist's establishment on the side of the street. I'm terrible at keeping things alive. But these kept me alive.

"All that glitters is not gold" and "Not all who wander are lost" are both quotes from J. R. R. Tolkien's *The Lord of the Rings—The Fellowship of the Ring*, to be specific. However—and specifically—"All that glistens is not gold" comes from Shakespeare, who might have taken it from the twelfth-century monk Alain de Lille, who himself may have stolen it from Aesop. Thanks, Wikipedia.

The lovely man named Samuel who got the fact that *In the Shelter* is a bit of a long letter about language also is the publisher and editor in chief of the *Marginalia Review of Books*. You'll find it online. It's delicious.

Lorna Goodison, "Reporting Back to Queen Isabella," in *Oracabessa* (Manchester: Carcanet, 2013). Lorna Goodison served as the poet laureate of Jamaica from 2017–20. In 2019, I decided to read everything she's (currently) published. It made for a marvelous year.

Frederick Douglass's words about the Irish are collected in many different manuscripts, but this quote came from Noel Ignatiev's magnificent monograph *How the Irish Became White*, published in 1995 by Routledge.

Nuala Ní Dhomhnaill was the Ireland Chair of Poetry from 2001–3. Her comments on how language was denied women poets comes from the book *Cead Isteach / Entry Permitted: Writings from the Ireland Chair of Poetry*, published in a glorious bilingual edition by the University College Dublin Press in 2017.

The "There is no present or future" quote from Eugene O'Neill is from his play *A Moon for the Misbegotten*, which premiered on Broadway in 1947. Leon Uris used the same quote as an epigraph for his 1976 novel *Trinity*.

The line quoted from Gerard Manley Hopkins is from his gorgeous poem "Spring."

Acknowledgments

All of the stories in this book are true. That is not to say that all of the facts are indisputable. Sometimes it's because I'm trying to shelter someone's identity, other times it's because of the shadow of forgetfulness, and still other times it's because you should never interrupt a good story with a fact.

Most of the stories are stolen, but as I've learned, that's a good thing.

There are many people to thank.

I learned to love language in a family of love and stories. Thanks to my parents, Paddy and Ann, my siblings, Áine, Seán, Ciara, Méabh, and Niall. And to the smallies and the outlaws, who have expanded the table of love.

Thanks to PD, grá mo chroí.

I used to write letters to imaginary friends when I was younger. Now I'm older and the letters are imaginary but the friends are real. There is no greater gift than friendship. Thank you.

I still talk to myself, though. I learned that from Gandalf.

To the people with whom I worked over the years. Your photos are still on my wall. Your stories are still in my memory. Your friendships are still in my life.

Acknowledgments

I meet every Tuesday with friends around a table of food and talk. Tuesday Group is an irreplaceable sacrament.

Thanks to the Corrymeela Community—for shelter, challenge, life, action, and friendship.

Thanks to Krista Tippett and all at the On Being Project for being a guiding light for so many years—and now beloved friends and colleagues.

To Katherine Venn, senior editor at Hodder & Stoughton. Her careful reading, editing, and questioning—together with Friday afternoon laughter meetings—influenced every page. And to Lil Copan, from Broadleaf, for her careful readings of readings.

Thanks to the supportive and inspiring individuals at Hodder & Stoughton, Hachette Ireland, and Broadleaf Books—whose love for language is a gift and a call.

To the people of the imagination, the people who shape ideas, curiosity, and life with poetry, radio, fiction, and essay. I cannot imagine my life without the shelter of your craft.